Finding Your Lighthouse

A Leadership Guide to Navigating Change

Jenean Merkel Perelstein

Tree of Plenty Publishing

Flagstaff, Arizona

Finding Your Lighthouse: A Leadership Guide to Navigating Change

Tree of Plenty Publishing
Flagstaff, Arizona 86001
www.alchemieacademy.com

Publisher's Note: This book is designed to provide accurate information in the subject matter presented. No guarantees are made about expected outcomes. Client results are individual and used to provide examples only. The author/publisher shall have no liability to anyone who claims loss or damage, caused either directly or indirectly by the information in this book. Client names have been changed to protect privacy.

Cover Design: Julie Sullivan shinecreativeindustries.com
Cover Portrait: Dawn Kish dawnkishphotography.com

To book Jenean Merkel Perelstein for a speaking engagement, visit AlchemieAcademy.com/speaking

Library of Congress Control Number: 2017901719

Paperback ISBN: 978-0-692-84294-2
Digital ISBN: 978-0-692-84295-9

For Scott

Thank you for believing in me.

CONTENTS

Preface

However difficult life may seem, there is always something you can do and succeed at

~Stephen Hawking – Theoretical Physicist

We are all powerful beyond our own understanding. We are individual battery packs of power and yet so many of us choose to live life as if we were victims to life's every want and whim. In truth, we are everything but victims in this world. We are buzzing balls of potential and success - when we choose to create it for ourselves.

This is a book about leaving mediocrity behind. It is a guide for those of you who want to have the feeling of control again. This is for you who want to stop being reactionary to your life and start creating a more powerful version of yourself, no matter what kind of change you are trying to navigate through.

I am excited to share with you what I have learned along the way on my journey toward standing in my strength. It is time for you to do the same.

~

About 16 years ago, my husband and I were driving home to Flagstaff from a trip to Phoenix. It was late at night and we were keeping each other awake with deep conversation. We were discussing a topic that set me on a track of inquiry that continues to this day.

We wanted to know: Why were there people in our lives, who got everything they set out to have, be, or accomplish? Why were there some people who had the Midas touch? What were they doing? Did they have some kind of superpower? Were they special in some way? What made them continually lucky, in all their endeavors, when others were not?

We knew people like this and wanted to know if there was anything we could do ourselves to be more like them. We wondered if there was a way to arrange for our lives to be as golden as their lives were.

Then again, we also knew some of the other kind of people. The people who seemed to block their own success at each and every junction. It was interesting to us that some of our acquaintances found ways to sabotage opportunities that otherwise seemed within reach.

I should note here, that these acquaintances of ours who did not achieve success at all like their counterparts, have equal access to the big 3 success indicators in life: wealth, power and prestige. They were in similar socioeconomic strata as our lucky friends and because of this, it occurred to us that perhaps there were things they were *doing* that kept success out of reach.

This discussion intrigued me. If it was possible that the lucky and successful people were doing things to invite success in their lives, I wanted to know how! Likewise, if there were things that the truly unlucky of our friends were doing to sabotage their success, I wanted to know how to avoid those particular bits of nastiness and keep them from creating obstacles in my life.

At the time, I was teaching socio-cultural anthropology at Northern Arizona University. I am blessed to have chosen a discipline that teaches me to look at the world through the lenses of cross cultural comparisons and pattern recognition that became so valuable in unraveling this mystery. In fact, I still use the principles of anthropology in all the coaching that I do today.

This meant that I embarked on a study of inquiry into the language of success. I began to look for ways to understand why some people moved through life with tremendous ease. I wondered why some people treated the kind of obstacles that would stop mere mortals in their path as if they were adorable little speed-bumps and glide easily over them.

I also began to research what people did when they blocked success in their lives. I found clues to the underworld of self-sabotage and the ways that we knowingly and more often, unknowingly get in our own way even when we are actively trying to succeed.

I looked for clues in other cultures, in other timeframes and in other disciplines. My study took me across several continents as well as several subcultures in our own backyard. I broke beyond the comfort of my home discipline of anthropology and began to ask my questions within the fields of psychology, business, behavioral economics, quantum physics and the neurosciences.

The resulting body of work is introduced here for you to discover.

I would love to be able to tell you that, knowing these secrets, I took a linear path to quick success in my life. But the truth is that it started sporadically as a hobby. So naturally, my results matched my efforts. In my spare time, I gathered information as I could. It was not until several years after embarking on my quest for knowledge about success that I really began to take it seriously.

When the lightbulb went off for me, I was working as CEO of a great youth non-profit. Everything was going swimmingly. I received ample validation from others that my life was exactly where it should be. Everything was perfect. I had a wonderful, loving husband; two beautiful, healthy, young boys; a gorgeous house and a job leading an organization with a fantastic mission. My life was complete.

Except it wasn't.

Now, I am the kind of person who loves to share my exuberance with everyone. As an extrovert, I share energy with the people around me and one of my favorite pastimes is to elevate the energy in the room with my joy. When someone asks me how I am, I really do love sharing a hearty "great" with them as I attempt to light their fire with my own spark.

So, that was how I knew that something was wrong. When people began to ask me how I was, I began to tell them I was "fine."

What? Fine? This is where the alarm bells went off and red flags were hoisted in my mind.

The message became really clear when close friends of mine asked how I was and I began to well up with tears. I was anything but fine.

But the problem was, I did not know why.

All around me my life looked great. On paper, I was living the dream. But the fire inside me had gone out. I had lost my mojo and I felt like I was on a hamster wheel living out someone else's life. I couldn't figure out what went wrong.

Then the shit really hit the fan and I got sick. Many months went by without knowing what was wrong or how I could treat it and my life began to look pretty bleak. I was trying to save the children of my community at work and did not even have the energy to take care of my own two boys at home. It was as if the conductor of the Fast Train that I was on told me my ticket was no longer valid and booted me right off.

Something needed to change.

I left my big-girl job and dedicated my life to change. I knew that what previously had been a hobby needed to be a serious priority if I was going to become healthy and feel like myself again. I also knew that I was going to have to change my diet, exercise and stress levels. Most importantly, I was going to have to capture my old, more vibrant way of seeing the world if I was going to get better. It was no easy task set before me.

I dove into this work with the enthusiasm of someone who had nothing to lose. My lifestyle of stress had me heading to the grave and I needed to find ways to become more successful at any cost.

My collection of articles, notes, books and studies provided me comfort and direction as I began the healing process. Some techniques which I tried on for size simply did not fit. They ended up on the cutting room floor of my office. But other techniques intrigued me in their ability to help move me more firmly onto a path of success. I could see the change happening for me as I played with each individual test, and I became committed.

Next I played with combinations. Which of the exercises provided the best results when combined with others? What combinations were most powerful? I looked into redundancies and culled my collection further.

As a final step, I tested the order of my experiments. I wondered if some components to this work became more or less powerful depending on when it was performed in the sequence of events. Indeed, there was a vast difference, and as with the combinations, I found the sweet spot.

As I began to heal myself, I took on clients who needed help with marketing their businesses and attracting clients. Since much of this inner work was making a profound difference in my own life, I peppered in some of my newfound wisdom for my business clientele. What I learned was that the more I worked with them on their inner game, the better their business results were. I began to see profound changes in people who had previously dragged their feet perpetually. All of a sudden, they were getting out of their own way and achieving more than ever before. I was floored by their outcomes and I started to see what was really happening.

You see, it really did not matter how good the marketing plan I gave them was. Because I still had clients who were churning out mediocre results with excellent plans. What made the difference was helping them work on their inner game of success. And then, "Katie, bar the door!", they were off!

Eventually, I began to insist that anyone I worked with, whether they needed a strategic direction or a marketing plan, must go through this inner work first. I did not want to waste anyone's time now that I knew how to maximize their success.

Through the years, I have continued to tweak the process and build on the scientific evidence supporting my program's components. I have used the exercises that I am sharing with you here to help people achieve amazing success. The long list of outcomes my clients have achieved include: starting businesses, reaching sales goals, losing weight, repairing relationships, growing clientele, achieving abundance and freedom, finding a soul-mate, traveling afar, and gaining respect and recognition in their fields.

I am pleased to be able to share this body of work with you because, if I have learned anything throughout this journey, it is that I simply love watching people successfully navigate change and begin to stand in their strength. Even the most successful among us have room to grow. It delights me to guide you through the process.

Introduction

If your actions inspire others to dream more, learn more, do more and become more, you are a leader.

~ John Quincy Adams – Sixth President of the United States

Congratulations.

I have no idea what prompted you to pick up this book. Maybe you've got big changes in your life to look forward to, or maybe you simply need to do a little fine tuning. Whatever the reason, you are in the right place. I am thrilled to be sharing this ride with you and I promise that it will be rewarding.

Before we dig deep into the lessons ahead, I want to share with you some ideas for success that will help you make it through this journey. These are principles of leadership that have helped guide countless pioneers through treacherous adventures; whether through unknown lands or local boardrooms. I have taught these principles in many forms throughout the years and they are worth keeping our eye on as we endeavor to challenge and change our results moving forward.

Lesson 1
Trust Yourself

One of the strongest muscles you can strengthen for good leadership is to build your awareness - both externally and internally.

We, as humans, have done an excellent job at learning how to control our environment around us to create useful and comfortable lives. We use tools, produce food, and enjoy such extravagances as efficient transportation and electricity. We have done this by finding ways to control our surroundings.

But what happens when we reach the limits of the environment around us that we can actually control? Nature has a way of controlling us. When we have farmed too much, the soil becomes depleted. When we waste resources, we must do without.

Have you ever seen this play out in someone's leadership before? They begin by controlling their environment and become successful because of it. Their control over forces can lead to favorable outcomes for a good long time-until the day that it does not work anymore. For some, their need to have control *over* a given situation versus working *with* it will lead to their eventual demise. There is such a thing as too much control.

As you look to your surroundings and what new areas you want to affect change around, notice when the forces of nature are asking you to work *with* it instead of trying to control it. Good leaders will know the difference. They'll know when it's time to stop pushing and reassess the situation.

One of my favorite sayings is a Chinese Proverb.

> *When the winds of change blow, some will build walls and others will build windmills.*

Constantly ask yourself if you are building walls or windmills. Are you using your external environment to help create change *with* you or are you trying to shore up the foundation to keep external forces at bay? I guarantee you that if you attempt to control too much, too often, the winds of change will blow you off course.

The other kind of self-awareness that I find necessary for good leaders is of the internal sort. In fact, you could say that the bulk of my life's work lies in this arena. I am a huge fan of studying what I believe is the most important topic in life: yourself. In fact, as an anthropologist, I take very seriously the true meaning of the word *anthropology* - *anthropos* from Greek, meaning human or man, and *ology*, meaning science, branch of knowledge, or study of such a thing.

Hmm, the study of man. Sounds pretty exciting eh? And what if that study were of the particular man (or woman, certainly!) that is YOU? Now we're talking.

It is along this vein that becoming aware of the machine that is you, is of the utmost importance. To be perfectly clear, while I will spend some time with you discussing your physical self, most importantly, I want you to know about your mind, your heart, your guidance, your beliefs, and your behaviors that *make* you achieve your results in life. We will dig deeply into these questions in this book, but for now I want you to focus on the boundaries of your strengths.

Naturally, it is important for all leaders and successful individuals to have an inventory of what they are good at. This brand of self-awareness will continue to be necessary no matter what new endeavors you approach. The more you know about your strengths, the more efficient you are likely to be. Efficiency, by the way, is one of my favorite tools in excelling in life.

But what many people also fail to do is to take note of where their strengths end. People will commonly think that they are very good at something only to reach the outer limits of their abilities and fall flat on their faces.

You have certainly seen this. This is the gal who knows she is a natural story-teller only to try to bullshit her way through a meeting and gets in over her head. Or the guy who knows he is good at negotiating only to get crushed by his competition who he underestimated. This is also the CEO who runs an amazingly successful mid-size company then fails at scaling into an international phenomenon.

While these are all excellent growing opportunities, they can also be warning signs that tell you that you need to know where your strengths *end.*

It is up to us to know when we must surround ourselves with people who are better than we are at the things we need to do. Trust me on this, if you want to upgrade your outcomes, you must be willing to upgrade your teams of people who compliment what you do well. In order to do that effectively, you must know your strengths, and also when your strengths have reached their limit.

Lesson 2
Trust the Fear

It has taken me some time to learn how to trust the fear that I experience as I reach for something new, but these days I work with it all the time. As a matter of fact, I am rushing up against this test right now as I stretch myself to write this book. I am having to knowingly lean in to the fear of being uncomfortable.

In order to change your outcomes and results, you will need to do things differently. As I will outline later in detail, it is your brain's job to keep you safe; read: the same. Part of being comfortable means doing things as you have always been doing them. But as we all know, doing the same things over and over will undoubtedly yield the same, or similar results.

Breaking out of the comfort zone means making choices that will, by definition, make you *uncomfortable*.

Discomfort could show up for you in many different ways. For me, I often feel it as a physical symptom in my body. Every time I have really pushed beyond what feels normal for me, I feel a bodily discomfort that is so unsettling I want to shake it off. In fact, that is what I do to work through this. In the spirit of full disclosure, in the process of writing this book, I will periodically get up out of my chair, pace the room, and shake my body like a wet dog.

While this does not necessarily cure my case of the bad-feels, it settles my nervous system enough to plough through for a while longer.

But that's just me. Everyone *feels* change differently. Some people will be so excited they cannot sit. Others will feel like there is an elephant sitting on their chests. What is it for you?

Part of self-awareness is to know what your body, mind, and/or spirt will do to you to keep you "safe."

In trusting the fear, you must know it when it shows up, see it for what it is, call it out, and then find a strategy for carrying on. Yes, I said call it out. See it for what it is and call it a name if necessary. "I see you, fear. I know you're trying to slow my progress. I know you want me to sit on my couch and eat bon-bons and drink beer. I'm not going to. I'm going to carry on and do amazing things!"

Whatever you do to it is up to you. For me, shaking like a dog does the trick - for a while. Knowing if physical cues show up for you will be necessary in changing your outcomes, and in doing this work you *will* be challenging your comfort zone. But magic does not happen for people who stay comfortable all of their lives. It happens for those of us who periodically shake like a dog.

Lesson 3
Trust the Momentum

It is important for you to keep traveling in the direction of your dreams every day. While I will go into much more depth about strategies on how to get this done later in the book, I mention it here because this is one of those things that natural leaders just DO. They DO. They work toward it and they know, with all of their being, that doing is coupled with trusting. When you trust that movement is taking place even when you cannot see immediate results, you keep going.

We all know that success builds more success and it sucks when you cannot see that you are being successful in any way. There may not be any external validation that what you are working on is having an impact. In fact, much of what we get rewarded for in life is delayed. Sometimes we build foundations for a good, long time before anything resembling the house we intend to build takes form.

Be patient. Be mindful. And keep going. Your ability to trust the momentum in what you work toward could just be the difference between you and the next guy who quits four feet from success.

Have you ever seen the potential in someone else rise *almost* to the surface? And you know they are nearly there? And you can smell success for them but they give up before reaching it?

Some people have a knack for this specific brand of self-sabotage. In fact, some people actually *specialize* in it. They get all fired up with energy and gumption at the beginning of a project but then they lose the faith in the momentum that is happening on their behalf. They forget that they have set anything in motion and believe that they are starting anew each and every day.

I like to think of someone pushing a huge boulder down the road. To begin with, things are difficult and any movement at all is painfully slow. You might have to build up your leg muscles and really push your shoulder into it before it will even budge. But eventually it will. It may start to move slowly at first; in a game of inches. But before long you get it rolling. It is here that you need to be careful not to stop! If you stop, even for a little while, you will have to heave your shoulder into the great rock to get it going all over again. But if it gets rolling along, even at a slow pace, you can *keep* it going without as much effort.

This is the principle I want you to think about as you embark on a journey of change in your life. Trust that you are making a difference, even if you cannot see evidence of that yet. Even if that perfect relationship has not shown up for you. Even if the promotion you want seems three layers of bureaucratic tape deep, when you are actually working on the principles I am going to share with you in this book, you must trust that momentum is on your side.

Lesson 4
Trust the Magic

When I tell you to trust the magic, I realize that some of you may roll your eyes at the concept. I promise that I will have much more to say about legitimizing magic as the book unfolds. At this point however, I want to implore you to remain open to the magic and serendipity that is more certain to find its way to you on a frequent basis when you begin the work in this book.

We are going to be purposefully inviting success to come and grace our lives and with that will come an abundance of magic…if you are open to it. If not, it won't.

I have a running joke with my clients. We talk about the "You are not going to believe what happened…" phenomenon. It usually begins around our third session (later, you will learn why) when they come into my office or call me on the phone all abuzz. Magic has ensued in their lives and they cannot wait to tell me. This is why I love what I do and why I want to share it with you. I want for each and every one of you reading this book to write me and tell me about the magic that is unfolding around you. When you get really good at deploying these tools you will begin to feel as if you possess your own magic wand. It feels as if you can orchestrate the Universe around you as it brings what you have asked for. Or sometimes, the Universe brings you things beyond what you have asked for and beyond your wildest dreams.

If you begin this work lacking a sense of wonder or magic it certainly will not come for you. I will explain the science behind much of this work as it is substantiated in my own field of anthropology, and also in psychology, the neurosciences, and even quantum physics. But there will be some things that I simply cannot explain. I will try to be frank when those instances arise. And they will. There will be times when I do not know why it happens, but I know through experience with working with countless others, that it does happen.

Have you ever wanted something and felt certain that you knew exactly how it will show up for you, only to be completely surprised at its arrival in a whole different way? Have you ever experienced a "miracle"? This is the kind of magic that I am speaking about.

I like to remind myself that there are many things in my life that I do not fully understand but that I trust to work just the same. When I pick up my cell phone to call a client on the other side of the country, I trust that I will be connected even though I have no idea why or how that happens. I am quite okay with my ignorance of such technology. But I know that it still works without me being filled in on the secret.

That may happen for you here and I am asking you to fully embrace it. In fact, trust that it will happen and look for it to happen. Magic happens for all of us when we believe it is ours for the receiving and we delight in its gift.

Lesson 5
Trust the Systems

Trusting the systems has been the hardest won of all the leadership lessons for me. If there is an area of self-sabotage that I excel in, it is right here. I will let you in on a little secret.

You see, I suck at being an employee and I have known for a long time now that I have to make it as an entrepreneur, no matter what. The main reason for this is that I really do not like to be told what to do. I LOVE my freedom. And I believe that as a business owner who values freedom above most everything else, I have to protect it from the kinds of systems and structure that companies and bureaucracies hold.

You see, what I did not know at the beginning, and what I want you to learn without the heartache that I experienced, was that, in fact, structure sets you free. And herein lies the source of my problem.

You have to put in place and embrace systems and structures so that you can experience freedom without being reactionary to life.

It is not a punishment, as I wholeheartedly believed when I began this work. It is a benefit. When you put systems and structure in place you do not have to think about every move you make. You have more time, and you have more energy and brainspace for the things you value most.

I avoided structure in order to hold tightly to the idea that I could go day-drinking with my girlfriends on a Tuesday if I wanted to, but without structure I had to be completely reactionary to everything that came my way on every other day. Once I embraced the idea that I could put systems into place that would enable my business to run and *gain momentum* without my eyes on it, I gained freedom without feeling guilty. I knew that I had earned it and that things would not fall apart in my absence. I realized that putting my shoulder to that rock anew, following each time I wanted to take a day to myself, was too exhausting.

So, I began to learn from the experts. I got coached and mentored and I learned systems that I could trust with my best work. Oh, the irony. I had developed my own system and expected my clients to follow along while I was bucking the system, so to speak, at every turn. It did not work.

Not only did I fail to get enough done before I lost momentum again and again, but I was sending messages loud and clear to the universe that systems were not to be trusted. I created obstacles for myself from my own imagination and mindset. It was not until I put my trust in a coach's expertise, a coach who could guide me through the steps toward efficiency, that I began to see the light.

Please believe me. Following a plan does not take away your freedom, it gives you more of it.

~

You are now ready to embark on a journey of change with me and to embrace your greatness. I am excited for you and for what outcomes you will achieve as you invite success and welcome abundance.

This book is broken into four segments, each segment providing corresponding exercises.

The first segment is titled **Searching Within**. Here we will analyze the results you have today to best uncover where hidden beliefs or other agenda have been getting in your way. While we will not need to go into detailed past histories, I have found that ignoring this piece of the adventure keeps people in habit loops of self-sabotage that they were never even aware existed.

The second segment, **Affirming Purpose**, is where you will learn to identify your lighthouse, or where you want to go. I will discuss common goal-setting pitfalls, how to get around them, and most importantly, how to remain connected to your purpose along the way.

In **Inviting Success**, the third segment, you will learn exactly how to navigate toward the change you want to achieve. This is a hands-on approach to changing the results you achieve through changing yourself. You will be able to replicate the tools you learn in this section to achieve amazing outcomes in nearly any aspect of your life.

And finally, in **Welcoming Abundance**, I will teach you how to keep your hard-won success from slipping through your fingers by embracing a real lifestyle of success. It is in the mastery of these lifestyle tools where you can stabilize the inconsistencies of lack and abundance in any area of your life.

As you work through this book, I invite you to purchase for yourself a beautiful blank journal where you can write down your thoughts, your lists and complete your exercises. The more inviting the journal, the more likely you will be to complete the work. It will be powerful to have your entire growth journey in one place where you can return and reflect. Give this gift to yourself.

Join with me now, and begin the process of navigating change for success.

Searching Within

Chapter 1

A Case for Anthropology Or, A Very Good Place to Start

Never believe that a few caring people can't change the world. For indeed, that's all who ever have.

~Margaret Mead – American Cultural Anthropologist

One of the best decisions I ever made in my early adulthood was to travel. I spent some time going to school in London, traveling Europe, living and working in Bavaria, and traveling extensively through India and the Middle East before hunkering down for grad school. It was through these journeys and adventures that I fell in love with the discipline of anthropology and formed the basis of what ultimately became the programs that I teach to clients around the world.

There are two concepts that are central to cultural anthropology and happen to be strikingly important to understanding where we need to begin when we want to navigate and affect change in our lives.

Remember, if you want the results in your life to be different, you must reverse engineer the process and look at what is causing the results you have today. From there, you can change everything that informs your actions so that you may achieve better, stronger results. I want for you results that are more purposeful toward what *you* want instead of reactionary to what the world around you wants you to have.

The first of these anthropological concepts is understanding the difference, and indeed being able to recognize when you are being *culturally relativistic* versus *ethnocentric*.

Cultural relativity is understanding a slippery concept of what is "right" *relative* to your own culture. It is understanding that actions and values must be evaluated within the context of that specific culture, and not seen through the lens of your own personal actions and values.

To take a very simple example, when I left Europe for my first adventure in India, I knew I wasn't in Kansas anymore before we ever got there. Our flight path gifted us a layover in Damascus, Syria where we switched planes during a three-hour layover. The vast difference between what I experienced in the airport in Munich, Germany and the airport in Damascus, Syria had my head spinning.

The Munich Flughafen was clean and bright and new. Everything from the metal detectors to the toilets shone with a sense that *alles* was in *Ordnung.* While there were some European differences, things made sense to my Western-wired brain.

When I landed in Syria though, nothing looked *right.* Women were covered in clothing from head to toe and there was an utter lack of toilets altogether. Instead, I was introduced to my first of many holes in the ground that I was to squat over to do my thing. Curiously, the area around the hole appeared to be made of dirt even though we were on the second floor of the building.

When it was time for us to go through security, I was escorted out of line and taken to a small screened off room by a woman in full burqa. There, she patted me down gently and made sure I was not hiding anything in my bra.

I was thrown. "This is what is normal here," I thought. It took specific brain power to remind myself that what I was seeing was not "weird" or "bizarre," which was my first reaction. Rather, it was considered completely normal within the context of the culture I was in.

I was no stranger by then to experiencing different ways of life. I had already lived in England and Germany for a couple of years and was seasoned in such oddities as driving on the left side of the road and tipping the woman in the public bathroom who gave me three squares of toilet paper.

My lay-over in Syria marked the beginning of understanding that life could be vastly different beyond the adorable oddities I had experienced in other, fairly similar western countries. My perceptions of right and wrong were challenged and I experienced a true epiphany of understanding what was relative to the cultures I visited.

Incidentally, a subsequent, longer trip to Syria revealed the most generous, loving people I have met. We were treated with a level of hospitality there that has yet to be matched in my global travel experiences. Given recent events, I mourn the loss of many of the archaeological sites we visited as well as our ability to return.

Contrary to the idea of cultural relativity is when we do put our judgment onto another way of doing things. This is called ethnocentrism.

The ethnocentric traveler is a crass one. Perhaps you have seen the "Ugly American" insisting that someone in another country speak English, or refusing to wear long pants when it otherwise offends a foreign host. Ethnocentrism represents the worst of ourselves when we insist that our way is right and morally superior and the different way of doing things is wrong.

I should stop and point out that it is easy for us to say that as moral and compassionate human beings we always see things through the eyes of relativity. We like to think we would never behave from a perspective of ethnocentrism, but it does not always manifest as such a simple decision.

Take for instance, the idea that some cultures consider eating dog meat a perfectly normal way of subsisting. As I write this, my chocolate lab is curled up a few feet away and the thought of eating dog meat affects me viscerally. That is because my brain simply cannot reconcile something that is so deeply ingrained as being *wrong* and I want to fight to keep it that way.

Or take, for example, the idea of female genital mutilation: a practice in some cultures. In those cultures, it represents the rite of passage into womanhood where labia get sewn together and sometimes the young woman's clitoris is removed. Is my abhorrence to this cultural practice pointing to a human rights violation or an ethnocentric viewpoint?

Ethnocentrism is often a complicated issue as we attempt to affect change in our globalized economies and naturally, is studied extensively by anthropologists around the world. But what place does it have in personal and professional development, you ask?

Good question. You see, I have found that it is absolutely imperative for us to be in touch with the judgment we place on the values, behaviors, attitudes and beliefs that we have adopted. That judgment informs our outcomes. Likewise, if we were to adopt new and improved values, behaviors, attitudes and beliefs, they will lead us to new outcomes. We need to challenge any mistaken judgment or ethnocentrism we may have.

This discovery can be one of the first of many ways we uncover where we may be self-sabotaging our success. If we believe that our own way of doing things is more rational or perfect than another way, we are likely to dig our heels in the sand simply because of our addiction to our own version of "right."

I want you to begin to think of your new and improved self as having a different set of values and beliefs from your current self.

In addition to cultural relativity and ethnocentrism, the second concept from my home discipline of anthropology that reveals our self-imposed obstacles to success is another perspective exercise. When we experience something outside of our cultural norm, there are two possible ways that we view what we see. Do we take the *etic* perspective or the *emic* one?

The etic perspective is the easier of the two to adopt. This is an awareness that as we see another culture or a different way of doing things we observe it from an *outsider's perspective*. That is, we are aware of our differences as the observer. It is the easier perspective because we are used to applying comparisons and contrasts to describe what we see.

When I experience another culture or country I can easily identify what they do and how their culture operates by explaining the differences between my culture and theirs. My culture has coffee shops on every corner, theirs has tea stands. My culture does laundry in washing machines, they wash theirs on a river bank, and so on.

What is more difficult, however, is to view cultural norms and beliefs from the perspective of an *insider*, or the emic perspective. It includes looking at ourselves.

The emic perspective requires us to take note of what is ordinary and familiar. Taking this view is very difficult for us because the usual becomes invisible. When something occurs with regularity our brains have the ability to filter it out so that we no longer notice it. For instance, if I were to ask you what you are seeing right now, you would probably tell me about the view of the room or landscape in front of you. Maybe there is a table, or a bed, or a person there with you. What you probably would not make note of though, is your own nose.

You see, barring an unfortunate accident or birth anomaly, you can always see your nose in your field of vision. But since it is there with such regularity, your brain filters it out of what you experience, thus changing what you "see."

When an anthropologist goes to understand a foreign culture, it is valuable to gain the insiders perspective, the emic view. This is because a person familiar with a given way of doing things can unfold important information for the outside researcher. But we must always be aware of the limitations of self-discovery.

Understanding this concept is imperative in embarking on a journey of change and growth because we will need to see clearly what is happening in our own lives. I want you to see your results as having been formed from your culture of one, and understand them from both the emic and etic perspective.

Incidentally, this concept unfolds why it is important for even the most successful among us to have coaches in our lives. The highest-level athlete or CEO still operates partially from behaviors and beliefs that are hidden from them. Working with a coach can help provide a much-needed etic perspective to round out their awareness.

I am not just saying this because I am a coach. I have lived it deeply. I cannot tell you how many times I have been bogged down with a limiting belief or practice, one that keeps me in a rut or actually makes me revert backwards, only to have my coach reveal an obstacle that was right in front of my face. For me, the humbling moment comes when my solution is a technique that I teach on a regular basis to others whose self-sabotage I *can* see. But like the nose on my own face, I looked right past it.

With these ideas on board, we can do as Maria von Trapp says, and simply start at the very beginning. However, a problem often arises when we do not really know where that beginning is.

Problems of self-discovery often occur below the surface where we cannot really see them. We know that our minds often filter out what we usually see and what we judge based on our perceptions of normal.

An issue arises when we do not do an accurate account of exactly why our outcomes and results are the way they are. Often people start a program of change beginning from where they are today, ignoring what got them there. The problem this creates is that people can look past the underlying beliefs that cause their self-sabotage in the first place. This results in status quo outcomes.

To be clear, I am not a big fan of the need to go back to your childhood reliving all your painful memories in order to move forward. However, it is helpful to interrupt patterns of self-sabotage by inventorying your results based on the values, behaviors, attitudes and beliefs that have informed those very results.

Imagine for a minute that a colleague has invited you to a party at their in-law's house and hands you an address where you have never been before. If this house is in your own hometown where you have mastery over the location, you can probably find it simply by being clear on where the destination lies.

This is how most people approach personal growth. They figure out where they want to go and chart their course between where they live today to where they are going.

Well, that is just fine and dandy if you have a crystal-clear image of where you begin.

But what if you are handed an address to someone's house while you are visiting a strange city? You would probably need to know both your destination *and* where you are. Then you can map out each step of the way to get there, taking into consideration all known road-blocks that are likely to get in your way.

It is the same when you want to change your results by creating a new you. You must know where you are starting from by uncovering those areas of your life that are clouded by culture, hidden beliefs and bad habits to navigate this journey toward success.

Chapter 2

Our Brains at Work

Cognitive neuroscience is entering an exciting era in which new technologies and ideas are making it possible to study the neural basis of cognition, perception, memory and emotion at the level of networks of interacting neurons, the level at which we believe many of the important operations of the brain take place.

~John O'Keefe – Nobel Prize Winning Neuroscientist

In order to make lasting changes in our lives we need to make changes in our brains. Luckily for us we now know that our brains are *plastic*. That is, they are ever changing, and just because we have connections in our brains that compel us to behave in a certain way today does not mean that we are destined to do so forever. The old adage, "you can't teach an old dog new tricks" is a false cultural snub that keeps us tied to mediocrity: it is simply not true. You most certainly can teach a dog of any age new tricks, and we can teach ourselves as well.

I became interested in the brain research that creates the foundation for my work back when I was working as the CEO of a youth non-profit. I was studying about how pleasure centers of the brain become activated when people give philanthropically in the same way that cocaine and chocolate activate the brain. Just as all roads lead to Rome, many different stimuli lead to pleasure, and your brain does not really care if it is a destructive stimulus or a socially uplifting one.

I was fascinated with this idea and wanted to know more about the brain's response to different activities. I embarked on a research project of my own. My research led me to the neurosciences and I became hooked while learning more and more about how the brain works.

Particularly interesting to me were the studies that were conducted by the National Institutes of Health about what happens in the brain at the exact moment when we make a decision. Scientists were interested in how we choose during the decision-making process.

What they found fascinated me and informed my work for many years.

Scientists suggested that only 20% of the decision-making process was being filtered through our rational brains. That is, only one-fifth of our decisions were based on a logical process.

We are all familiar with making a big decision in our lives by sitting down with a T-chart putting pros on one side and cons on the other. We also faithfully do the research necessary to support a plan that "makes sense" based on which decision gives us more benefit. We will even use statistics to rationalize our logical decision by all means necessary.

But we have all felt it, and we have all been there. Our list will be heavy on the cons side telling us not to do the thing. But like the beautiful young teen in the horror movie who inquisitively opens the closet door while you are yelling at the screen telling her not to, something compels us to act otherwise.

But what is it? If 20% of the decision-making process gets filtered through our rational brain, does that mean that the other 80% gets filtered through our *irrational* brain?

Not exactly. At least not for everyone. The other 80% of our decision-making process gets filtered through another way. That is, through our emotions.

Because of this we sometimes behave counter to statistics and rational thoughts. When our pleasure centers are emotionally triggered in opposition to logic, we feel compelled to decide in favor of what will maximize pleasure and minimize pain.

This was fascinating for me to learn while I was in the business of fundraising and running an organization whose success relied heavily on persuading people to become volunteers. By using an emotionally-driven appeal, sprinkled with logical rationale, we could be more successful in our efforts.

Likewise, when I left my job in the non-profit world and took on marketing clients, the 80% to 20% decision making studies became key in developing effective client attraction plans. This is helpful in our market-driven society because my clients are interested in influencing buying behaviors.

But those studies were already about 10 years old and research has evolved since then. Today, thanks to improved technology in how we study the brain, we have learned more about how our brains operate in the last ten years than we were able to learn in the previous 100 years. New and exciting studies are being conducted all the time that inform us on how (decisions) and why (motivation) we do the things we do.

One of the more exciting standards to evolve out of this body of knowledge comes as an update to the decision-making research mentioned previously. Modern studies refining this work tell us that instead of a break-down of 20% logic to 80% emotion, the line should rather be drawn at 4% logic to 96% emotion. And instead of labeling these your rational brain and your emotional brain, scientists now realize that this is the difference between your conscious brain at 4%, and your subconscious, or unconscious brain at 96%.

Let's take a look at what this really means for us. It is here that our tools for success in change and growth really lie.

Our conscious brain, the small part, is what you are using right now to make sense of what you are reading. It is the part of our brains that we are most familiar with. Believe it or not, it is the part that we most often activate when we move through our day in the Beta brainwave frequency (more about brainwave frequencies in chapter 12). Our conscious brain operates slower than our subconscious because it does not have as much information to process - less than 200 bits of information per second. While 200 bits per second may seem like a lot, and it can be, it pales in comparison to the information the subconscious processes.

Our subconscious brains operate much differently. Since the role of our subconscious brain is to maximize pleasure and minimize pain, it is on a constant lookout for what we need, or in fact, what it thinks we need in our lives (Let me take a quick time-out to acknowledge that yes, I will be anthropomorphizing your brain, and as a heads-up, I will do it with the Universe later on as well - like the occasional cuss-word, it's how I roll). Your subconscious brain wants you to be happy, but the rub is that it has to process *millions* of bits of information every second to find that happiness. Your subconscious brain becomes the filter that determines exactly what information gets to your conscious brain. Note that research varies on exactly what constitutes a *bit* of information as well as how many bits of information get processed through your brain. Just know that the subconscious brain processes a shit-ton more than the subconscious brain.

So, the question becomes, why do we filter out what we do? And why do the things that get through the filter into our conscious minds and ultimately shape our outcomes, get through in the first place?

The answer to this lies in our beliefs.

And where do beliefs come from?

Beliefs are enculturated. We get our beliefs from our families, our society, our cultural norms and our experiences. We learn early on the rules about what is "supposed" to help us maximize happiness and minimize pain, and we follow that script as we learn to navigate through the world. Beliefs are embedded as subtle nuances within everything we do, such as how to get dressed in the morning, what we eat and the language we use.

The problem with enculturated beliefs is that they often steer us in the exact opposite direction from our desired results. Our belief-informed filters are sometimes set to bypass important information so it does not get through to our consciousness. The hidden secret is, the information that we need to achieve successful outcomes in our lives is usually there for us all along. We therefore create barriers to success all by ourselves by bypassing, or filtering out, the exact information that might lead us directly to success.

Think of it this way. Imagine that you are finally being rescued from a desert isle after having been stranded there during a nasty storm (As a kid from the Seventies, this is one of my favorite fantasies). Surprisingly, on the island with you are *millions* of the exact things, ideas and bits of information that you will need to achieve your goals once you are back home. But the boat that rescues you can only accommodate fewer than 200 of these potential success items; the same amount of information that gets into your conscious brain.

You have grabbed the things that you have been taught might help you become successful; the things you *believe* will help you. But if they are the same items you have always used to guide you toward success, you just may end up stranded on a desert isle again. Why wouldn't you? It stands to reason that if you want to change your ability to reach your goals, you would need to change the things, thoughts, ideas and information that you travel with.

It is the same if you want to change the things, thoughts, ideas and information that get filtered into your consciousness from your subconscious. You need to change on the level of your *beliefs* so that the right bits get filtered through (or taken on the boat, to reconstruct the analogy) creating better outcomes.

There is another bit of information that neuroscientists agree is necessary to understand in this work. That is, that we will always, always (read: habitually), be compelled to behave by direction from our beliefs.

Let that sink in for a moment. If you have a belief, your brain, or more specifically the 96% of your subconscious brain, will MAKE you behave in a way that supports that belief. Additionally, your subconscious brain is consistently looking for evidence that its beliefs are true. Do you know where it finds that evidence? In your behaviors.

If it sounds to you as if I am talking in a circle, you are correct. This is the powerful feedback loop of your brain that creates habits.

If you have a belief, your subconscious mind will compel you to behave as if that belief is true. Then, when it observes you behaving in a corresponding way it says, "Hey! I knew it! This belief must be true! Why else would you behave in such a way?" and it embeds the connection between your belief and behavior even deeper.

If, as you may have surmised, you were to use the 4% of your conscious brain to behave differently than your beliefs dictate, then your brain would make you feel uncomfortable. When you feel uncomfortable and experience stress, you are more likely to revert to habitual behaviors, finding yourself acting once again, as if you were dictated by your old beliefs.

This is why those of us who try to use willpower, or our conscious brains, to change a habit often fail.

Say you wanted to eat salads for two of your three meals every day as you embark on a health-conscious lifestyle change. You consciously planned for it, shopped appropriately and made a bold declaration to yourself and others that this was going to become a new habit.

You did really well the first day. Your conscious brain is doing fist pumps in the air at your success and you are feeling powerful. Then, on the second day, your colleague invites you to lunch with them and you think, "Why not? I've got this!" and, you go and order a salad. Except that you end up eating all of her fries as well. Then at dinner, you sneak a few chips from the pantry but are still proud of yourself for eating all those greens.

By the third day you are starting to get fed up with salads and opt for a veggie burger at lunch, justifying it as a better choice than the quarter-pounder you normally would have eaten. At dinner, you eat your kids' left over macaroni and cheese.

Day four is a disaster, and now you feel like an utter failure as salads, and the plan to eat them, become a distant memory.

What went wrong? Well, the initial plan was a good one. The problem lies in the fact that in this example, you are only using your behaviors to change a habit. That means that you are relying on the power of 4% of your brain, all the while ignoring the more powerful 96% of your subconscious brain that may have had other ideas for you.

Let's explore this more deeply. Perhaps it is possible that somewhere in your brain you have a belief that salads are not very filling. Add to that, you might have a belief that there is not enough protein in salads and you will become lethargic in the afternoons because of it (this is a false belief, by the way). Maybe there is even a deeper, insidious belief somewhere in you that suggests that being 10 pounds overweight is safe because you do not want to draw attention to yourself, which is something you secretly fear.

If you have any or all of these beliefs, and then try to use your conscious mind to affect change without rewriting new beliefs that support your new behavior, you will fall prey to the power of your old habits. In times of stress, we resort to our old habits. And subversively, attempting to change a behavior causes stress.

I would like to give you a couple of examples where attempting behavior change and not beliefs change led to poor results in my work.

Many years ago, I was doing program evaluation for a Non Governmental Organization (NGO) in Bangalore, India. The mission of this organization was to do HIV and AIDS prevention with vulnerable populations in this city of 8 million people. However, they were experiencing poor results and could not figure out why.

When I arrived in India, the members of the NGO were throwing their hands in the air saying that they were handing out hundreds of thousands of condoms in the marketplaces where sex workers operated, but were seeing HIV incidence in those areas rise.

It did not take long for me to fully understand their problem. I went to the markets with my translator, Nagaraj, to interview some of the women there. Among other interesting things I learned, (seriously, you should buy me a beer sometime and I'll tell you some tales) one young woman confided that they did not understand how the NGO workers expected them to swallow one of those nasty condoms every time they had sex.

Herein lies their problem. You see, the good folks who gave the sex workers condoms were asking them to change their behavior. "Use a condom," they would say over and over again. But the problem was not in the sex workers' behavior. They tried to use a condom but it was wildly unsatisfactory to them and caused a measure of stress (and probably some gastrointestinal issues as well). In times of stress they reverted to their previous beliefs.

Included in their long list of beliefs were probably messages such as: I need to work to feed my children no matter what; I do what my clients want me to do; and the biggie- condoms work to protect me by swallowing them.

Until the NGO embarked on an educational program to address the *beliefs* of the sex workers that caused barriers to change, they could hand out a mountain of condoms without their efforts making an iota of difference.

For another example, fast forward several years and I was working with a marketing client in the United States who was a massage therapist. He began working with me because he was concerned that if he did not get more clients in his practice, and soon, then he would have to give up his entrepreneurial lifestyle and go get himself a J-O-B; something he really did not want to do.

But week after week I would give him client attraction assignments and he was not completing them. Mind you, these were not highly complicated or taxing strategies either. He simply was not following through with what I mapped out for him.

Finally, after suspecting that his sabotage was being self-inflicted by some hidden beliefs, I asked more about his inner motivation. Eventually, after some deeper probing, he finally admitted to me, "You know, Jenean, I'm afraid that if I do all of these things that you're asking me to do then I'll be working so much that I won't have enough time for myself and my family."

He agreed that the program I was sharing with him would work. He was sabotaging because his hidden beliefs created fears when he realized that the techniques would work too well.

To overcome his sabotage, we mapped out exactly how much he wanted to work and how much time he wanted for his family. To keep in control of his schedule, we created a trigger for when he would switch from client *attraction* to client *maintenance* and we created a belief for him that it was possible to have power over his schedule.

The beautiful thing about knowing when our subconscious brains are trying to keep us "safe" is that thanks to the relatively new study of neuroplasticity, we know that we can change our brains and rewire positive, more helpful beliefs into our lives. When we are purposeful about creating beliefs that support the outcomes we design, instead of being reactionary to what we have inherited from our culture, we can achieve success.

Chapter 3

If Being Positive Was All It Took

Keep your face to the sunshine and you cannot see a shadow.

~Helen Keller – American Activist and Seer of the Beautiful

Your current level of thinking equates to your current level of success. We know now that much of how successful we are has to do with what has been hard-wired into our subconscious brains. But what about the thinking we have the most control over, occurring in our conscious brains?

Let's take a minute to talk about our thoughts and the effect they have on our lives and our outcomes. Just as the neurosciences play a role in planning a successful route toward better outcomes, the field of quantum physics opens a door of possibility to us that should not be overlooked.

Almost 100 years ago, Neils Bohr and his colleagues pioneered the "new science" of quantum physics. A field so outrageous that many people today prefer to dwell in the land of Newtonian physics simply because they cannot wrap their brains around what the new science tells them.

The very basics of quantum physics comes from the idea that at the subatomic level, everything is simply made up of energy. That is, when we gained the capacity to magnify the particles that make up atoms, we see that all that is left to observe is energy. This mind-blowing principle tells us that everything we perceive as solid matter: the trees, your hand, your table, is all made up of rapidly moving energy.

When we take this craziness a step further we learn that it is our perception of reality that makes it so. But these are details for another book. What is important to know here is that everything around us is made up of energy. And one of the most potent forms of energy, according to modern quantum physicists, is thought.

Thomas Kuhn, who teaches us about paradigm shifts, said that, *"all the significant breakthroughs were breakthroughs with old ways of thinking."* We have to question the way that we see the world so that new possibility can show up for us. How amazing that these new ways of thinking about where power and change come from, back up our ideas of what is possible.

Behavioral scientists tell us that we experience somewhere in the neighborhood of 60,000 thoughts a day. And 95% of those thoughts are habitual.

Think about what I discussed in the previous chapter about habits. If 95% of what goes through our brains, and affects our behaviors, is habitual, and was encoded for us by other people who may or may not have our best interests at heart, are we really living our lives on purpose?

But let's go back to thoughts for a minute. Quantum physics tells us that energy is attracted to its like frequency and to other particles that it has "entangled" with before. Entanglement, in the field of quantum physics, suggests that if particles of energy have "met" before or have been in contact before, they will forever be affected by one another. These principles remind us to keep our thoughts, as they are pure energy, aligned with positive frequencies.

It is interesting to me to look at the intersection between the highly new-age-ish forms of woo woo, and the hard science that is vetted by peer review and publication. I had always been a bit turned off by the simplistic messages coming out of the field of personal development telling us to think positively, simply because they had utterly lacked reasoning for me.

"What if I don't want to monitor my thoughts to always think positively?" I had considered. But after learning about how our thoughts affect the wiring in our brains and how they attract energy of like frequency, I have bought into positivity wholeheartedly.

This is one of those areas for me where I know that science backs up my reasons for thinking positive on a regular basis, but there is also a magical component to it that I experience but cannot fully explain. I believe, after several years of studying the effects of positivity, that we somehow become "rewarded" by the Universe for feeling good. Perhaps I am tapping into the field of energy that quantum physics still struggles to explain to non-experts. Whatever it is, I know without a shadow of a doubt, that positivity aids in my efforts to change my results. I have seen countless times how it accelerates the results in my clients. It simply cannot be ignored in this process of changing your brain to allow for a higher level of greatness.

Thinking positively is the only thought framework from which to leap into the realm of personal and professional development. I will open up other reasons for doing so later on, but for now, it is important to stress that the inspiration birthed from a position of positivity is powerful when someone is motivated to change their brains and change their frequency.

But positive thinking is not enough.

There has been some unfortunate backlash from the heightened popularity of such change catalysts as the movie, The Secret, and other Law of Attraction (LOA) and manifestation introductions that are popular in our culture.

Don't get me wrong, I really loved that movie, and I am a huge fan of LOA, but I have seen people out there get in trouble with it. They learn that thinking positively will allow them to vibrate on the frequency of the things they want and then the things that they want will want them. While I do believe this all to be true, the holes in this theory come when people believe that this is *all* they have to do.

Sadly, there are those out there who have sold the farm in the promise of good things to come, only to sit on their couches all blissed out with positivity and then do nothing of action to get the ball rolling in their favor. Then, when they watch the bills pile up and their dreams gifted to other people, they blame the system and sink into a bitter version of their former selves.

Because it's not that simple.

Yes, I will tell you ten ways 'til Tuesday that being positive and vibrating on the frequency of what you want is the way to go, but there is so much more to creating and navigating change than positivity alone. Change does come to people who are positive and joyful more than it does to people who are negative and sad. But it also comes to those who actively work toward rewiring their brains and changing their outcomes. And you have to work at it.

For example, if you want to own a successful business but do not actually want to work on the business, you may want to re-think about what it is that you really want. More about learning how to do this effectively will follow, but please believe me when I tell you that you cannot be lazy in the name of positivity and expect greatness to come.

On the other end of the spectrum, I should mention that the positive viewpoint is not Pollyannaish at all. I have known those who embark on a course of change, knowing that shedding fear and negativity in lieu of positivity and joy, is the first step in attracting the solutions to their problems. Only then to be met with scorn from other people in their lives who think that being positive in the face of adversity is ignoring the reality of their situation.

Yes, some of you have very troubling problems that you are trying to overcome. No one is telling you to ignore them completely or to belittle their importance. But let me ask you this; by constantly worrying or fretting over the stresses in your life, aren't you giving them too much energy? Are you perhaps feeding the beast who is attempting to keep you down?

Have a good talk with the people in your life who see things differently. Perhaps you can bring them around. I will talk more about the influences of people you surround yourself with as you go through a period of change later in the book, but for now, start the conversation. Maybe you can help them uncover some of their limiting beliefs and add more positivity into their lives as well.

Give positivity a try. Catch yourself when you come from a place of negativity and note when it really does not serve you.

Begin to see what can happen when you experiment with raising your level of positivity. Do as the quantum physicists suggest and raise the frequency of the energy that is YOU entirely with the quality of your thoughts.

Chapter 4

The Value of Our Fears

We can easily forgive a child who is afraid of the dark; the real tragedy of life is when men are afraid of the light.

~ Plato – Greek Philosopher, Founder of the First Institution of Higher Learning in the West

At this point in your process through this work, after dissecting your values, attitudes, behaviors and beliefs about different areas of your life- and committing to thinking positively, topics may bubble to the surface for you about where in your life you may be playing small. What areas of your life are you *not* living up to your potential? Do you feel uncomfortable in your body when you think about a certain topic? Could this be resistance to change coming from your subconscious brain that is trying to keep you safe?

It is common at this point for my clients, after analyzing their beliefs, to begin to achieve clarity on where they have been playing small and holding themselves back. At this point I hope you are aware of some of the limiting beliefs that have been holding you back as well. I am confident that if you are reading this book you are committed to changing those beliefs. I am also confident that you can achieve the kind of outcomes that you want when you are ready to break through any kind of resistance that comes your way. This includes overcoming the beliefs that do not serve you.

But before we begin the process of re-wiring your subconscious for better results, I want to share with you another mental process that I find holds some people back - that is, the attachment we have to our fears. Did you know that the fear of falling and the fear of loud noises are the *only* two fears that we are born with? All other fears are layered on by our experiences. Just as we can learn to be afraid of something, it is possible that we can learn to be unafraid as well.

It is important to have a complete inventory of what you are afraid of. Now, I know you must be thinking that I am crazy after having spent an entire chapter talking about the importance of positive thinking and now I want you to dissect the fears you hold. And you are right. I do not like to spend much time adding energy to things that do not serve us in the end. However, if we are going to move past the areas of our life that are getting in our way or blocking us, we need to know what they are. Fear-based blocks can become major impediments toward positive change if they are left unaddressed.

The interesting thing to note about fears and how they relate to changing our opportunities to succeed is that fears can provide different kinds of motivation for different people: some good and some harmful. It is extremely important for you to know which category you fit into with each of your fears, the good or the harmful.

For instance, if at the top of your list is a fear of failure, ask yourself if this fear is true for you. Think for a moment if this fear is simply inherited from years of messaging from others that ultimately became embedded in your hidden beliefs. More often than not, being afraid of something has simply become a habit that is holding you back. You believe you *might* fail and that is terrifying because society tells you it must be.

Think for a moment about people you may know who do not have a fear of failure and so continue to take risks in their lives and are richly rewarded because of it. The only difference between you and them is that the story of the future they tell themselves has a different outcome than yours.

That is a key component here. Before you attempt to *do* anything, its outcome is fiction. You truly have no idea what will really happen and any speculation toward the negative will only hinder your ability to actually achieve it. If you use your powers of fiction for good instead of evil you may be rewarded with one of two things: success, or a learning opportunity.

When you think of the question, "is this fear true?" ask yourself if you are playing out a script that enables negativity instead of empowering positivity. It is often your choice. Perhaps there is an opportunity for you to hold a belief that says that everything positive is possible instead of a belief that everything negative is possible.

But that is just one example, of one kind of fear that does not serve you in your quest toward greatness. There is another response to fear that may give you different results. Consider the affect that fear had for Jeremy.

Jeremy is a client of mine who owns a small business. When we began working together he was having a difficult time scaling his business to the next level. He did not believe enough in himself and his abilities as a leader to drive his business where he wanted it to go. When I interviewed him about his fears, topmost in his mind was a fear of not making enough money to support his wife and children.

I asked him if this fear of lack was true, because often for people it is not. But for him it was. "Yes," he said. "I could lose everything within months if I make a wrong move."

Here is the difference between Jeremy's fear of lack and the fear of failure I mentioned above. He was right. In this instance, it would be ridiculous arguing with him about it being fiction. For Jeremy, his fear was true. It was a real possibility if he were to make poor decisions in his business. The thing that made it perfectly clear to me that it was different from the types of mistaken fears listed above, was his *reaction* to the fear.

You see, for Jeremy, the fear of not making enough money was a driving force motivating him to keep going. He did something different with his fear than many people do with theirs; he used his fear to fuel his quest.

For many people, fears are crippling. When they are faced with the prospect of what scares them they stop in their tracks and do not budge forward. Because of this, it is important to know if you have a fear that is keeping you from change and growth. It is also important to be clear on when your fear is useful in your pursuit of greatness.

I am going to generalize by genders here, knowing that, of course, there are exceptions. I have found that many more men use fears to motivate them than women. I am sensitive to my brethren in gender studies who may have a more in-depth explanation for this phenomenon but, suffice it to say, it is valuable for everyone to think deeply about their fears personally, and know how they affect *you*. Be aware of what action to take, if any, the next time you feel affected by your fear. Perhaps now is the time to choose to let your fear go.

Write down your fears in your journal and note whether they serve you in charting your course to greatness. Pay particular attention to what happens in your body as you think about these fears. This will inform you on whether you need to change the beliefs surrounding them or keep them where they are.

~

Before we embark on the next section where we get down to work on changing our outcomes, there is one more inner inventory in your journal I want you to make.

How committed to this process are you? Are you really ready to make a change or is this one more personal development book that will fire you up today, only to be forgotten on a shelf next week?

I know, I have been there. I cannot even begin to count how many books I have read and not been really committed to or taken any action from. In fact, it is this idea that has kept me from putting my work into book form for many years. Much of what you read here (and so much more) is in audio form with a corresponding workbook entitled *Internal Alchemie: The Welcoming Abundance Blueprint*.

When I first began coaching from the Blueprint I also sold it to people as a home study course. I can tell you that the people who completed the course with a coach (either with me or one of my Licensed Internal Alchemie Coaches) had far better outcomes than those who simply listened to the program and completed the workbook on their own. While it is completely possible to have great outcomes, and some have, those with just the program were less committed and so achieved fewer results.

I have mixed feelings about writing this book for the same reason. I am positive that if you were to follow the principles in this book, you will achieve amazing results. But will you?

Ask yourself right now if you are the person who reads a book, comes away with a few good ideas, but never changes your habits. Or are you tired of living with the same old mediocre results and are ready to actually *do* something about it. If you are truly ready, then this book is for you. If you are not truly ready, be real with yourself and go find something that you enjoy and stop spending time on things that you *might* do. Let me bless and release you now to your own devices.

It may actually do more damage than good if you step into this endeavor timidly: without commitment or conviction. It has the possibility of providing you with more evidence of a limiting belief. You might believe more deeply that you "are not the kind of person that can change," or that "you don't finish anything," or that "you're too lazy to do the work." We all have limiting stories in our heads to overcome. But if you are ready; truly ready, to change your outcomes to receive more success and growth in your life then please, commit with me here.

I would like for you to write a letter to yourself in your special journal outlining your commitment. Tell yourself what you are willing to do and how much time you are willing to spend on honoring change in yourself. Tell yourself that you believe in YOU and your abilities. Remind yourself that change is possible and success is your birthright. You deserve greatness, and while I can tell you multiple times, it will not mean smack unless you hear it from the one person who truly has authority to tell you: YOU.

Once you have written the letter, sign and date it and review it often. Remind yourself that you are participating in a process, and even if it gets difficult somewhere in the middle, you will be able to review how far you have come by revisiting what you have written in your journal.

Affirming Purpose

Chapter 5

Scientific Doodling

This world is but a canvas to our imagination

~Henry David Thoreau – Essayist, Reflector of Nature

In this next section, we will be discussing the importance of becoming clear on what you want and the value of knowing *why* you want what you want. I will share with you methods of how to set these goals for yourself so that you actually reach them and ward off the monsters of self-sabotage.

I recognize that some of you already have clarity about what you want. You may know now, or have known for a while, exactly what has to happen for you to feel successful. Others may be questioning if you want the "right" things or even worry about not knowing what you want at all. You may find yourself in that camp of those who, like me early in my journey, "feel fine" and simply want that fire inside you to return, but you are not sure how to go about doing it. Hang in there. It is in this section that we get you back to Mojo-Ville.

But first, how is that journal of yours going? Are you keeping up with it? Did you write your commitment letter? How did it feel to get that down on paper? Do you feel somewhat relieved to have the question answered of whether or not you will follow-through on your intentions this time around? Are you just *interested* in change or are you really *committed*?

Sometimes when you have doubts about taking on a project or starting something new, those thoughts are left to swirl around in your subconscious brain looking for some resolve to anchor them to. If you have enough of those unmoored thoughts chattering on in the back of your mind you will, without a doubt, create a sense of overwhelm for yourself.

One of my main roles as a coach is to help people tame their overwhelm. This means looking for times and areas in their lives where it may creep in. I help them create systems (remember those?) to quiet the chatter in their subconscious so that they can focus on the things that are truly important to them.

One area where this commonly becomes a problem is when people design their lives around the need to multitask. Do you know the true definition of multitasking? It means doing nothing well.

When we jump from task to task there remains part of our attention on the one, two, five, or more other things that are left in the background. Each of these hanging tasks creates questions in your subconscious brain such as, "I wonder when I'm going to get back to that other task" or "if I leave this too long without doing it I'll be screwed." This means that the part of the mind that is attempting to focus on the particular task at hand is compromised. Your attention is spread too thin to do it well and your emotions are hijacked by the not-knowing of the jobs left undone.

This does not mean that you should never switch quickly from task to task. Some jobs will certainly require it. Goodness, I am the mother of two teenage boys, I am a task-switcher by necessity.

The cure to being bogged down by overwhelm lies in calming the questions in your subconscious. If you have a plan, or a system to get back to your secondary and tertiary tasks, your subconscious will say, "Oh, ok. You've got this. I don't need to worry about it on your behalf because you have a plan to get to it later without fail."

Have you ever been unable to sleep at night because too many to-do items keep crashing around in your head? We have all read the articles from experts who tell us to get up from our beds when we cannot sleep and write down the thoughts that are keeping us awake. The reason this works is that it provides a plan for your brain to work on and quiets the questioning of whether or not you will blow it off, or actually get it done.

As we move through this program, pay attention to the things in the background that you need to attend to. Write lists that remind yourself when you will get to these items. Pay close attention to the chatter in your brain that pulls your thoughts away from the task at hand and write about those thoughts to calm down the questions in your brain.

The excellent multi-taskers out there (and I know some of you are saying, "this doesn't apply me! I'm great at multi-tasking.") don't actually take on many projects at once, they are simply skilled at bouncing quickly between tasks without any kind of hangover effect *between* them that slows them down. You can get rid of the hangover before it begins by writing down the tasks you need to accomplish and then committing to them one by one. This way, your brain will not go searching for other things it should be doing while you are trying to focus.

And here lies the perfect time for me to bring up the importance of *writing* things down; on paper.

I am a huge fan of old school pen or pencil to paper. Heck, use a crayon if that floats your boat, but know that it is highly valuable to your brain. Writing helps you achieve your goals, especially when you hand-write them versus type them.

Anthropologists study a universal concept called *sympathetic magic* that shows up in nearly every culture. In sympathetic magic an item or word becomes a symbol that stands for something. Then, when you manipulate the symbol, it is believed that you manipulate the thing it stands for.

The obvious example of this is the dolls of the Voodoo religion. Likeness dolls are created with the belief that what happens to the doll will happen to the person the doll represents. Popular culture tells us that manipulating Voodoo dolls is necessarily a bad or harmful thing to do, but I will ask you to check your ethnocentrism here.

Because, if you think about it, don't you also use sympathetic magic in your life too?

Please stay with me here. I know that some of you have been enculturated into a religion that tells you that all magic is necessarily bad or the Devil's work. Magic, as I use it here though, is the scientific definition of a universally represented phenomena within the study of anthropology.

Do you wear or accept the wearing of a wedding ring that represents the circle of infinity and love in a committed relationship? Have you ever lit a candle at home or in a place of worship to represent a holy intention? Have you ever used a word or phrase to symbolize something you cannot see? These are all examples of sympathetic magic that are commonly used in our lives.

Your subconscious brain loves symbols. Remember that your subconscious is constantly filtering out millions of bits of information and has to do so quickly. Because of all that filtering, it has to categorize things as fast as possible and will use heuristics, or shortcuts, to do so. One of the ways we work with our brains to our benefit is to show it when something is important to us. This is the first way to manipulate the filters of what gets let through to our conscious brains.

When we write words, we are creating symbols. Interestingly, our brains will add a layer of importance to the things we make on our own because when they come from our own creativity, they evoke an emotional response. The more effort we put into the creation of a thing, the more important it is to our brains.

By physically creating words with intention, we tap into a kinesthetic bond between our bodies and our minds. The more ornately they are embellished, the more importance we assign to them.

When archeologists study the artifacts of varied cultures throughout time, another universal they note is the embellishment of utility items. Pots that are used for storing food will have designs on them, cloth is painstakingly dyed with beautiful color. The addition of artistic embellishment does not typically add to the utility of the item, but it does add to the emotional response we have in connecting with that item. It is suggested, and I truly believe, that the creation of art is a response to a human need.

Have you ever gotten in trouble for doodling in class? Or maybe you have received a sideways glance for drawing on your notes in a meeting. The dominant culture that tells us that we are not paying attention when we are doodling is just plain wrong. In fact, we are sending signals to our subconscious brains that this is important. So, doodle away. Add color. Add importance. The work you are doing here is for your success and your happiness. Help your brain pay attention

Chapter 6

You Are Unique

You are unique, and if that is not fulfilled, something has been lost.

~Martha Graham- American Modern Dancer and Choreographer

I know that if I feed you with particular information right now I can prime your brain into responding a certain way. Sounds manipulative, right? It is.

Studies show that when we are fed certain images or messages we can become more racist, tolerant, hateful, loving, lucky, unlucky, negative or positive. There is even evidence to suggest that if I prime your brain in a certain way, I can make you think as a visionary or from a detailed perspective.

For instance, if I were to show you a picture of a shady looking character, whose skin happens to be black, holding a gun and wearing a robber's mask and then had you take a profile test measuring how racist you are, your score would reflect a higher racist index than if I were to show you a picture of a black man in a business suit.

And it does not matter if you are black yourself. This level of racism can be manipulated for even the most compassionate among us.

There are also studies that show that people who believe themselves to be generally lucky will have better results on tests than those who believe themselves to be unlucky. We prepare our brains to respond to our commands, and if we are constantly feeding it with messages of negativity, we will get nowhere when and if we decide to try something new.

Right now, we are at the dawn of experiencing a new version of ourselves. So, we need to prime our brains into believing that we are all that *and* a bag of chips.

In the next chapter I am going to be asking you to set some goals for yourself. It is imperative that you come at these exercises primed from a place of thinking big and reaching for the outer limits of what you have achieved before, versus thinking small and staying in a place of mediocre results.

It is wildly important for you to be reminded of just how amazing you are. Remember, your brain needs evidence that a specific belief holds true. If you are about to embark on a new adventure, you need evidence that you are good at embarking on new adventures.

And no, I will not believe you when you say that you are not good at taking on new adventures. I am quite sure that you are and that you have simply forgotten. You see, culture, and our society around us does a very good job at telling us not to champion ourselves. Early on, we tell our children not to brag or boast about what makes us amazing. It is not a bad practice to keep us from boasting in and of itself, because it keeps other people from feeling bad about themselves in comparison. But we are so adamant about how awful arrogance and conceit are that we grow up warding ourselves from even coming close. Because we do not want anyone to get even the slightest sniff of conceit, we forget to champion ourselves - even a little bit.

Not only that, but we also deflect our greatness at any moment possible. Here is a script that I learned as a daughter of American culture. Tell me if it sounds remotely familiar:

Friend: Wow! You did a great job on your presentation!

Me: Oh, no. It was nothing.

Friend: Really. You were amazing just now!

Me: No I wasn't, stop. But you. You did an amazing job at your piece of the presentation.

You have heard it before. Any kind of compliment that comes our way not only gets deflected but actually negated. It is a game taught to us by our cultural norms and it does not serve us well.

The problem with this scenario is that as always, your subconscious is listening. It is constantly on the lookout for evidence to back up its beliefs. Then, every time you do something great and it hears you discount it, the belief that you are not so great is more deeply engrained.

Each time we deflect or negate a compliment our subconscious mind has further proof that you really are not good at doing whatever you just negated. Then the next time you want to take on a new endeavor, you will not have any evidence to provide your belief system that taking on something new is a good idea. You have taught yourself to forget what you are good at. Instead we are taught to remember only why we suck and why everyone else around us is great and capable of doing expansive, new things.

When we do not internalize our own greatness, we crave external validation. We actually need other people to remind us that we can do great things because we have forgotten our own power. Since others may have been championing you all along you might be used to it coming from an outside source.

But what is the problem with external validation? Well, for one thing, you do not really believe it. I am sure that my friends would lie to me to pump me up when I need it. Sorry friends. But really, I have seen you do it! And two, it is unreliable. You cannot expect a compliment or to be reminded of your greatness on your own timeline if you are expecting it to come from someone else. What if they are not around right now? What if they've got their own issues to be thinking about first?

That uncertainty leaves us with the scary realization that we have to become our own champions. We have to build ourselves up in ways that no one else can do for us. We have to prime our brains for greatness on a regular basis so that we can provide our subconscious with the evidence that we can do anything.

Believe me, you can. I have learned that people who are attracted to this kind of work always have successes under their belts. You do not get to this stage of life without them. You may have to spend some good time with yourself to unearth them, but they are there. Believe me. I am not just blowing sunshine for you, I know that will not work. It really is time to provide your own validation.

I have for you a three-step process involved with capturing your own greatness where writing in your journal is necessary. Please remember to add embellishments and doodles to your heart's content. Make it shine, because you will be rewriting your own story. You get to catalog what is possible for you while priming your brain to set goals from a place of success. You will have an inventory of your own successes any ole time you want or need it.

The first step in the process is to write down a list of all of the things that make you unique. You are a one of a kind person and the things that you are drawn to accomplish come from your own special you-ness. Please think about this holistically. That is, come at all of these questions from many different angles using varied themes to think about the question. Think of your uniqueness at work, at play, and within all the roles you adopt in life.

I do not mean to suggest that you need to be the only person in the world who has these properties or talents. But perhaps you apply a perspective in an original way or you regularly do something out of the ordinary. Look at the combinations your interests and talents make. For instance, I am certainly not the only Personal Development Coach in the business world, but I do not know of any who come at the study from an anthropological perspective. That makes me unique. What makes you unique?

Revel in the coolness that comes from being an individual as you read your list. Evoke the emotion of your strengths and send a loud and clear message to your subconscious that says, "I AM SPECIAL!"

Next, I want you to make a second list of what you have mastered in your life. What are you good at? Don't let the term "master" trip you up here. Please know that I am priming your brain for feeling good about what you have accomplished. I want you to feel good about it too.

Though I do not advocate for external validation when you could be telling your own story, I also recognize that we are trying to overcome years of purposefully forgetting what we are good at doing. If you need help making this list, ask a beloved friend to help you. You can use help with capturing the story, but once you have it from your friend, write it down and really take ownership of it. Make it yours. Internalize it in the way that tells your subconscious that you are serious about your awesomeness in ways that you have perhaps neglected for a while.

Are there commonalities between the two lists? Was it difficult to distinguish the two? That's okay. Use this as an opportunity to think about your greatness from different perspectives. Perhaps the intersections between the two lists can reveal something important to you. Trust your intuition to tell you if you need to pay close attention to one or more of the things you wrote down.

The grand master of all the positive-priming exercises that I recommend EVERYONE in life do is to create a success journal. This is a biggie folks, pay attention.

I want you to write in your journal ALL of your successes from as far back in life as you can remember. Write down the big, resume-style accomplishments and also the smaller things that you have done to overcome obstacles. In fact, every time that you can remember when you overcame a difficulty, write it in your journal.

Once you have back-filled your journal with everything you can think of from your earliest memories to today, keep them going. Make it a regular practice to write what made you successful today.

Even if that means writing, "today I woke up and brushed my teeth." Believe me, I completely understand how that can be a rip-roaring success on some days. The point is to remind yourself that you can succeed, even in areas that you may question from time to time.

Then, at any given point in time when you need to stretch beyond your limits to take on something new, you can read through your success journal and provide your subconscious with all sorts of great evidence that you actually believe. You know it is true because you are not going to try to pull the wool over your own eyes and fabricate lies in your own journal (right?). You can read it whenever you need to and not have to rely on someone else to boost you up.

Once you get the basics of your journal filled out, you will not believe how great it feels to read through it. You will feel so buoyed, it will seem like you have taken some kind of mood-altering drug. And you have. The pleasure centers in your brain will be activated by your own badassery (yes, my son assures me that's a word) and you will be ready to take on the world.

When you have finished these exercises, your brain will begin to filter looking for other things to write in your journal. Using these exercises to prime your goal setting viewpoint ensures that you will not be making a glorified to-do list- you truly will be reaching for what is possible for your next opportunity.

Chapter 7

Finding Your Lighthouse

Inside my empty bottle I was constructing a lighthouse while all the others were making ships.

~Charles Simic – Pulitzer Prize Winning Poet

It is truly amazing what you can accomplish when you set goals for yourself. So often, we float through life like we are in a boat in the ocean without any paddles. Some days the water is calm and gentle and takes you exactly where you want it to go. Other days the water is rough, with plenty of current and waves to make our journey treacherous. Other times the current leads us to a still pool forcing us to eddy out and get stuck in stagnant water.

Wouldn't it be better if we had paddles that give us some control over where we are going? That is what setting goals does for us. It provides us a tool to use to affect change in the direction we dictate. We become powerful over the external circumstances that try to set our course for us.

Sadly, some people live their entire lives never realizing that paddles were ever a possibility. They rejoice in the calm times (as they should!) and they complain about the rough times as if they had nothing to do with creating them or no way out of their situation.

But that doesn't have to be you. I want you to be purposeful over your life and live your life on your own terms. I want you to set the right kind of goals for yourself, in the right way, so that you can make beautiful, joyful change in the direction of your dreams.

Are you ready? (hint- this is just like reconfirming your commitment. Stop now and re-read your commitment letter to yourself)

I want you to imagine now that you're navigating your boat in the dark of night after having spent a very long time at sea. You know there are rocks and currents and waves in your way that you'll have to pay attention to, but you are comforted by the large, bright beacon of light that shines from the lighthouse on the shore marking the way toward the land that you've longed for.

That lighthouse is your goal. It is the final destination marking exactly where you want to be when you know that your goal has been reached, even though there are obstacles that may come in your way between here and there that will most likely steer you off course.

You see, everyone in pursuit of goals gets steered off course for some reason or another. It may be because you suffer from ADLS (Attention Deficit, Look Shiny!) and start working on something else for a while. Or maybe you get thrown off course because life lays obstacles in your path in the form of illness, or traffic, or impatient spouses, or arguments with your coworker, or any other reason that seems worthy of your attention at the time.

The problem with much of the goal setting advice out there is that often people do all the right things for getting clear on their intentions only to blow it completely when they veer off course. I want you to imagine from the get-go that you WILL find yourself off course. Allow for it so it won't throw you for a loop when it happens. If you have your lighthouse clearly defined, and you can see it even in the dark, you can always navigate your way easily back to where you need to be.

Incidentally, this is why, when setting a goal, I always tell my clients to let go of the *how*. So often people think about the things they want in life but immediately begin to fret and worry about how they could ever, possibly, maybe, probably not achieve it. They have primed their brains for failure before they ever left the harbor.

Several years ago, I met a woman at a party who embodied this concept. As we had just met, we were getting to know one another thorough the traditional means of asking how each of us occupied our days. She told me that she worked for the Park Service doing unfulfilling work. She said that she really wanted to get into conservation on her own terms but, "You know, with rent to pay and the job market how it is, it's just really not feasible to think that way."

This made me so sad for her. I could see that she was not even allowing herself to explore the possibility of what could happen if she were not bogged down by the job she didn't like. But as it works, as soon as she tried to problem-solve the how's, she got in her own way.

I am a natural visionary and it is common practice for me to dream beyond my means. It's how I escape when things become overwhelming for me. But for my husband, my big dreams sometimes cause anxiety. For him, he wants to know that my dreams are possible and wants to do what he can to make them come true. But that also means that he immediately begins wondering how on Earth we are going to pull off the next Merkel scheme. It has been an interesting dynamic for us for years and something that we have to specifically identify to keep it from being a problem.

But when we agree to let go of the how, we somehow always get there.

Here is how it works:

Go back to your vision of navigating your boat at night. Let's say that your boat has a light that illuminates the next 30 feet of water. Your lighthouse is 10 nautical miles away, but you can only see the obstacles that are directly in front of you.

What would happen if you were to direct your attention to what "might" be in the way two miles ahead? Could you be distracted from fully understanding the jutting rock that poses an immediate danger?

Assuming that you navigated your boat to starboard to avoid a danger in front of you that has been illuminated by your light, you now have the ability to see 30 additional feet in front of you. From this vantage point you do two things. One, you make a new plan of what to do in that 30 feet. And two, you stay mindful of heading in the general direction of the lighthouse.

What typically happens when someone sets goals is that they try to anticipate all the rocks and waves and currents and other boats that will be in their way all along their route. Then they chart their course based on what they know to be true or *assume* that they know.

While this is not a terrible strategy when you know exactly what to expect, I will go out on a limb here and say that if you are trying to reach for something new and great in your life you may not have any idea what could possibly get in your way. You are much better off starting to move in the direction of your lighthouse and redirecting back onto your course whenever you veer off of it.

That is why I want you to become crystal clear about what your lighthouse is. What goal are you trying to reach? Once you have that set, then do the first thing, and only the first thing in the direction of your goal. From there you will see the next logical step.

What if it happens to be the wrong choice? If you find yourself going in the complete opposite direction because of an intermediary step you made? Simply look at your lighthouse and course-correct. At least you will be moving and you can use the momentum of having started something. It is much easier to turn your boat back toward the light than to start anew.

Chapter 8

Order Up

If you go to work on your goals, your goals will go to work on you. If you go to work on your plan, your plan will go to work on you. Whatever good things we build end up building us.

~Jim Rohn – Business Coach Extraordinaire

What would you like? What would you want to change about your life, your results, or your experiences? Who would you like to be? What would you like to accomplish, and what things would you like to have? In other words, what will your order be?

These are some pretty big questions and are intimidating enough to stop some people abruptly from surging ahead toward greater success and joy.

Let's take a look for a minute at what you have already accomplished here. Go back to your journal now and revisit what you wrote down when we talked about analyzing your results through the lens of your values, attitudes, behaviors and beliefs, what comes up for you? Did something reveal itself as an area where you may be simply tolerating instead of thriving?

Think now about these areas in your life where you know you have left untapped potential on the table. Now ask yourself what it would look like if you did not have to worry about *how* you would change that aspect of your life. Can you identify areas where you have been held hostage by the *hows*?

Suspend, if you will, judgment on how crazy it may seem to overcome the gap of where you are today to where you want to be. If you know every step of the way on how to accomplish a goal I call that a to-do list. Just get it done. But, if you cannot figure out right away *how* it will all come together, then you have reached far enough to identify it as a goal.

I do not mean to belittle the great to-do list items that we all have. But if you can reach your most audacious goals that way then close this book right now and get to it. Sometimes the difference between the people who are getting shit done and the people who are not is that the people who are getting it done are simply doing it.

Profound. I know.

Seriously though, right here is where the rubber meets the road for many of my clients. Often, becoming crystal clear on what they want and honoring their visions by writing it down is enough to get the universal ball rolling in their direction. I cannot always explain it, but this is where the magic starts to happen. It is as if the Universe wakes up and says, "Ooooh, that's what you want? I've been waiting for you to figure that out. Here you go. Here are some possibilities and opportunities to help make that happen."

And that is when people burst into my office and say, "You're not going to believe what happened!"

So, now is your time. Read through what you have written so far in your journal. Sit quietly for a while asking yourself, "what would be possible if you didn't worry about *how* you would accomplish it." Spill it all out of your big, fizzy brain and put it to paper. Then, when it is written down, re-read your commitment. Remind yourself that you are in this to change your life, not stay with the status quo. Not stay with what you are already comfortable experiencing.

After you have written it all down, I want you to trust sharing your goals and your growth journey with someone else. If you are not working with a coach, then trust a close friend. Ask them to be a confidant and to hold your journey sacred as you work toward making yourself uncomfortable. Tell them that you trust them to be your champion.

I read an online article recently about how you are not supposed to tell anyone your goals so that you would be more likely to accomplish them. That is the biggest load of bovine crap I have ever heard. Keeping your goals a secret means coming from a *lack* mentality. It suggests that you are afraid of "jinxing" things by making them public, and you are just putting power into a negative outcome.

Remember that your subconscious brain needs you to take this seriously. If you want to feed your brain with the message that your goal is volatile to outside forces instead of you being in control of your outcomes, then go right ahead, keep it secret. But then you will have to watch yourself sabotage your efforts as you live out the belief-behavior feedback loop.

Trust in yourself to set big goals. Then trust in someone else. The more you say your goals out loud, the more you will hear yourself taking them seriously. Write them down and make them pretty and prominent. Visit them often and nurture them as you would a new friend or a house guest. Take care of them and you will find your brain working with you instead of against you.

At this point, some of you may be panicking, not yet knowing what your goal should be. For those of you in this situation, please know, it will be okay. While some people come to this work knowing what they need to do, they just need help doing it, others feel a sense of ennui that cannot be explained. They are not sure what will turn it around. If you find yourself in this position, take a deep breath and trust that you get to play too. I am going to help you discover your own lighthouse in the dark.

If you are finding yourself without direction at this point, let me spoon-feed your goal to you. Write this down: "I want to be happier. I want to experience more joy in my life. I want to feel fulfilled."

Because really, isn't that what all of our goals are about anyway? I think about the common goals that my clients set and play the "why" game with them. That is, if I ask them *why* they want more clients, or to create art, or to improve their relationship with their spouse, they would all say the same set of things. "I want to be happier, to experience more joy in my life, and to feel fulfilled."

Any one goal is simply the means to happiness. It is great to be specific if you already know that creating art or repairing a relationship is the means that you want to take to get you to joy, but it is not necessary for success in this process.

I once had a client named Emily who came to me under these circumstances. She was feeling as if the light inside of her was beginning to dim and she couldn't put her finger on exactly why. She was a very well-known artist, had a lovely home, family and friendships. The trappings around her suggested that she already had everything in place to make her happy. The fact that she did not own it and feel it deeply, made her feel even worse because she was layering guilt onto the doldrums she felt.

When it came time for her to set her goals she reverted to old patterns. She thought about what had helped her get out of a funk in the past. The problem was that her old stand-bys were no longer useful to her. I suggested that she put these very goals about happiness and joy as place-holders in the blanks of her workbook and to continue on with the remaining steps of the blueprint. Sure enough, by the time we finished our work together she had figured out the steps she could take to recapture her verve. For Emily, she found her happiness in pursuing a new medium of art. She learned new techniques and broke beyond a mold that she had occupied for years.

Another thing to consider in this process is how many goals you want to set for yourself at one time. I know that when you listed the areas in your life where you were playing small, some of you came up with several. It is okay to name several goals; many of us have more than one thing to work on. But if you find yourself in this position I want you to prioritize your goals and then work on them one at a time. There is power in your focus. While it is possible to work on many things at once, as some of my clients have done, I would really like you to focus on one issue at a time and know that you now have the tools available to you to repeat the steps for other areas of your life.

It is now time to talk about *when* to set your goals. Obviously now is the right time because you have just set yours, and embarking on a new program to reach a new level of success is always the right time to do it. But setting them once, never to revisit them again is where some people end up getting into trouble.

I want you to think about your goal as a living, breathing thing that needs care and feeding just like your favorite pet. Maybe your goal is not a cute, fluffy puppy, but rather is a fire breathing dragon, and that's cool. The point is for you to know that it is a dynamic being whose evolution and changes need to be recognized and honored.

My client, Allison, is a highly-driven woman. She is no stranger to setting goals and reaching them. For her, the issue was rather how to keep herself from taking on too much so that she had time to enjoy her current stage in life. When she and I began working together her goal was clear: she had recently developed new skills from a graduate program and wanted to implement them into her professional career. We worked on helping to prevent self-sabotage as she did just that.

But something happened as she worked through the exercises in this program. She began to develop resistance to her new skills goal and when she got really quiet and clear, a new pathway began to take form.

For Allison, digging in her heels and keeping to her original goal would have taken her to an unfulfilling place. I have no doubt that she would be successful in getting there, but it didn't *feel* right to her. She needed to adapt to her feelings and discover a new goal.

I hope you allow for this as a possibility as well. Occasionally, we all need to check in with our hearts to make sure that our goals still apply in the right way for us. We need to re-evaluate regularly and often to feel the sense of joy that comes from imagining our goals coming true.

I have found that revisiting the goal setting process anew every three months provides the right amount of time to make headway on something I desire without going too far down the rabbit hole if I am not heading in the right direction.

While it would make sense to practice this routine with the fiscal quarters, as many companies do, I prefer to set my goals with the quarters of the sun. I evaluate my progress on existing goals and look for the potential of setting new ones each Solstice and Equinox.

I find it very satisfying to align my business with the natural world. I find that we spend so much time indoors that we block ourselves from the creativity and inspiration that comes from our connection to the natural world around us. Because of this, I try to always know the cycles of the sun and the moon. I remember to look up to see what the sky is doing as often as I can.

Come to that, and this is a true side note, when was the last time you had your feet on bare earth? If you cannot remember, you need to. It is important for all of us to remember that we are a part of something bigger than ourselves. And without wanting to sound too Woo-Woo, I know that none of my really good ideas happen within the confines of my office walls. Inspiration is far more likely to strike when I am outside, walking my dog in the woods during my daily forest bath.

But back to setting goals with the quarters of the sun. There is another compelling reason to do it at these times that I have come to secretly enjoy. If you are following along with a calendar, you will recognize that the Solstices and Equinoxes fall about 10 days before the fiscal quarters. This allows me to get a jump on my own personal accomplishments before the rest of the world catches up. Call me competitive if you will, but I like being ahead of the game.

Perhaps it also has not escaped you that setting goals on Winter Solstice, sometime around the 20th or 21st of December, gives you a healthy lead on the New Year's resolution racket.

Yes, I obviously have a problem with New Year's resolutions. Though it is not an issue with the goal setting aspect of it at all. It is simply that over time, our culture has gifted us with new meaning surrounding New Year's resolutions. If you are a child of American culture, or even exist within the realm of New Year resolution setting traditions, you will know this alternate meaning: it means something to give up on by February. So few and far between are the successes that came from a January 1st declaration that it has become a huge cultural joke.

I think there are many reasons why people do not tend to follow through on their New Year's goals. Some folks might feel a bit pressured to set the traditional goal of losing 10 pounds even when they do not feel ready to make any life changes. Others set their goal once and never revisit or revise again, only to find it has become a distant memory before Valentine chocolates ever hit the store shelves.

I have found that stepping away from the tradition entirely allows me to break my bigger, long-term goals into manageable three month chunks. It has been amazing to see how much more I can accomplish since I began doing this.

It is also possible, if you are up for the extra challenge, to add a layer of intention onto your new quarterly goal setting that gives the Universe around you permission to give you help. By aligning your goals to the quarters of the sun, and asking for the Universe to help with this, you are invoking the powers of sympathetic magic in the same ways that agricultural cultures have done for centuries. Call it God, the Spirits or don't put a name to it at all. Either way, the power of prayer is there for you if you believe in it.

But if that seems too out there for your taste, simply writing your goals with clarity, and following up with the rest of the steps outlined in this book will help you rewire your brain for success.

Chapter 9

Live Life on Purpose

The purpose of life is to live it, to taste experience to the utmost, to reach out eagerly and without fear for newer and richer experiences.

~Eleanor Roosevelt - Activist, Diplomat, First Lady of the United States

Remember in the beginning of the book when I talked about the fire inside me going out? I felt like I had lost my mojo even though everything around me was humming along swimmingly. It was a terrible feeling and one that I recognize in a good many of my clients.

It is an interesting phenomenon that commonly happens to successful people who seem, by all accounts, to be on track with their lives. But they feel miserable, and then they feel guilty for feeling miserable because they cannot seem to come up with any good reasons *why* they feel miserable.

Sometimes they will even invent drama in their lives to reconcile the feeling they have in their external environment with their inner world. Have you ever heard of a mid-life crisis? This occurs when a big, messy slop of feelings plays out for people later in life and causes them to do some wild shit.

It is not a huge surprise really, if you think about it. We work hard to create mastery and control over our lives. All along we are waiting for that time when things slow down, get easier and we can coast for a while. But then it happens. We coast for so long that our lives become *boring*. Everything that happens in our sphere of influence is completely predictable and the excitement that we feel when we are growing toward mastery over everything has disappeared. So, what do we do? We create excitement, any way that we can, even if it causes us pain. Or if we do not, we feel like something is missing.

If this resonates with you, even just a little, the tools in this section will help reignite your internal flame and just might keep you from completely losing it.

Let's begin by uncovering some of the common mysteries surrounding motivation. These mysteries reveal what causes drama within us - sometimes without our even knowing it consciously.

People are usually motivated to do things for one of two reasons: inspiration or desperation. It is important for us to examine this now as we attempt to understand why we sometimes feel so terrible when we are working toward what we think is greatness.

Take desperation for instance. Imagine that someone is up against a deadline at work and the stakes are so high that they will probably lose their job if their project does not go perfectly well. This worker-bee is probably struggling from sun up to sun down to get everything done on time...or else.

Now, I want you to try to *feel* what it is like to be under such pressure. Really put yourself in the shoes of the worker-bee who has such a desperate timeline. Suck-Ville, isn't it?

Yet this is how most of us live our lives. We are pressured by external deadlines that rule our schedules and our prioritization. Our story becomes the "what if" of disaster flicks. We sometimes forget what we were working toward all along because we can't see anything but the blur of the world going by.

Counter that with an example of inspiration. Have you ever been so excited to go on vacation in two days' time that you cram five days' worth of chores into two? This happens because all of a sudden you have tapped into a power source you did not even know you had. Your thoughts and emotions about your tropical destination, or gathering of friends means that your attention is on *why* you are driven to accomplish so much. You are inspired, and you are not bothered by the nit-picky tasks that have to get done because you are compelled to be productive. You are being pulled by an invisible force to work harder than you normally would.

It is this same kind of inspiration that I would like you to feel when you move through your world on a daily basis. Unfortunately though, many of us have lost sight about what truly inspires us.

It's not that we do not get inspired at all. We click through the stories on the internet that show good Samaritans doing their thing, or puppies and kitties overcoming adversity. It is all very inspiring and we love it because it makes us feel good.

But one of the reasons why those stories are so popular is that we are desperate for feeling inspired. Do you see the irony here? We are lacking inspiration from our own internal machine so badly that we feel desperation when we actually seek inspiration. It is a poor place to operate from and one that is destined to fail.

We need inspiration to come from within us. Just like looking externally for validation in our own greatness is unreliable, so is looking for inspiration from outside sources. Those outside sources are not always there when you desperately need them to be. And even when they are, what if they do not work? What if a story that you read on the internet or see on TV triggers some other kind of response in you? What if your brain takes a negative approach to the otherwise feel-good story that you were hopeful about? Wouldn't you rather manufacture and supply your own inspiration?

The difference between those who are motivated by desperation and those who are driven by their own inspiration lies in their connection with their own purpose.

When we become unmoored from our purpose we begin to feel that same adrift, reactionary feeling that comes from not being in control. We feel, no matter how hard we are working, as if life happens *to* us instead of *with* us.

Most of us start with a purpose. We are driven to do the things we do for a reason. But the good parts of what we accomplish are also coupled with the things we really do not want to do, and our joy sometimes becomes clouded by the negativity of our work.

For some, purpose has not been present in their lives in a long, long time. When we are children, we are driven to do things because they feel good. We run, sing, laugh, take chances; all because we are drawn to the joy those activities bring us.

As we get older, our focus gets drawn to the consequences of our every action. Again, it is not our fault, per se. Part of learning how to control our environment around us for our own benefit means analyzing what works and what does not. Avoiding negative consequences is a good thing, but you know what they say about too much of a good thing. Too much focus on what could go wrong aids in disconnecting us from what could go right.

Sadly, if left to its own devices, our brain will first focus on the threat, seeing only what could potentially go wrong. Then our executive brain kicks in, and our secondary response will be to calm down. Hopefully. By then our nervous system has activated, creating a rush of stress hormones that we will have to overcome some other way.

For our next exercise, it is imperative that we all connect in a deep, powerful way with our purpose. Said another way, *why* do you want what you want?

At this point, for those of you who are paying attention, you may be inclined to gloss over this since I did kind of give you the answer already. Remember in the previous chapter when I said that we all set our goals to achieve a higher level of happiness and joy? Well, that is absolutely true, but you *must* do the work to get to the emotional, gooey center in some way.

I do not care what work you do, but if you cannot tie your work to some kind of mission that fires you up, you will eventually end up on the hamster wheel, feeling like each day is just like the other. The fire in your belly will dim and the colors in your world will cloud.

Take time out now to do two things. The first is to figure out how you can find purpose in what you do *today.* If you do not change anything at all about your life and the way you live it, you still need to tie it to purpose in order to keep out of the doldrums. Why do you get up in the morning? What compels you to keep going?

If your answers fall into the desperation category, hang in there with me - I have some tools later on in the book that will help.

If at all possible, find a thread of inspiration anywhere you can and blow it up like a huge balloon. Tell yourself that you were born for a purpose and then write down what that is. As you move through your day, tap into that purpose as often as you can and see if the lever of happiness moves for you.

But we are not on this journey to stay the same. The second part of this exercise is about the future version of you. While we do need to anchor ourselves to purpose today, I also want to make sure that as you think about setting your goals, tie them very directly to the answer of *why* you want what you want. Once you answer that, ask why again. And again. Keep asking until you run out of answers and *hopefully* end up with happiness and joy.

This script becomes your purpose. Say with me, "Jenean, I live my life on purpose." It is true. It is your birthright to live a purposeful life. It is imperative, if you are going to achieve a higher level of greatness, that you tap into this powerhouse of energy. Without it, you will continue to run in place on the hamster wheel of life. Time to get off and really live.

Inviting Success

Chapter 10

Your Own Version of Success

Not what we have, but what we enjoy constitutes our abundance.

~ Epicurus – Greek Philosopher

Successful people invite success into their lives *on purpose*. At this point in the game (yes, it is a game that is meant to be fun), we are going to get into the nitty-gritty of exactly how you rewire your brain to change your filters so that you begin to recognize the possibility and opportunity that exists all around you and use it to your benefit.

By now you have had a good look at what hidden beliefs may be getting in your way, what you really want to achieve, and why, exactly, you want to achieve it. Hopefully you have a good image of what you want to be, do or have when you have achieved success.

Let's take a minute to talk about success and what it means to you as an individual.

It is common for us to take a rather ethnocentric view of success and think that it means the same to everyone else as it does to us. But in fact, we could not be farther from the truth when we take that approach.

Our own definition of success is as unique as our own feelings. This is because it is actually the feeling of joy and fulfillment that bring about a correlation of success and abundance. It is not necessarily the possessions, power or prestige that we often think equates success. In other words, success is not a thing, it is a feeling.

This is one of those places that we can get royally screwed by the dominant culture surrounding us. If we take stock of what messages are given to us by Hollywood and by Madison Avenue alone, we will see flawlessly beautiful people with abundant resources all rocking this game of life. Every magazine, commercial, or sit-com we see provides us with examples, in one way or another, of how we are not enough, and how we are not living up to the standards of our neighbors or our culture.

Even if we consciously stand for the value that beauty and wealth do not equal success, our subconscious minds are getting bombarded with contrary messages telling us we are not enough. We must buy this beauty product to rid ourselves of "unsightly wrinkles"; or we must buy the latest holiday decorations to impress our friends and family this year, and not get left behind.

The truth is, I fall victim to it too. I certainly do not want to, but I do. My conscious brain tells me that my wrinkles are well earned and enhance my own unique beauty, but somewhere deep in my subconscious mind I sometimes fall prey to comparing myself with others. And the house? Oh, what tricky messages our brains feed us about the places we need to live in. I absolutely love my house. It is my sanctuary and we have done a good job of making a comfortable home for our boys. Is it perfect? Perfectly not! I am fine with entertaining while we are in the midst of home projects because I prioritize time with friends over maintaining a flawless home. Though even with strong convictions like those, in times of stress particularly, I sometimes feel like it is not enough when I visit a home that seems to "have it all."

When this happens, I am reminded to revisit my own definitions of success. Because you see, defining the things you want to have or be are not enough in this situation. It will not work simply to write down what you define as your own ultimate thing or experience. I have done that. What is helpful though, is to have clear guidelines, and then recognize when society might be feeding you a "success" that you may otherwise reject.

When I find myself wondering if I should buy the expensive eye cream or new tile for my kitchen, I remind myself of three related ideas.

The first idea I remind myself about is that if I feel I "should" do anything, it is by definition, externally motivated. When I feel a *should* coming on, it is a reminder for me to check in with my own internal guidance system about what is really important to me and not necessarily just what is important to other people. I do not ever want to lose my unique me-ness, just to impress other people around me.

The second check in with myself concerns the idea that it could be that yes, I really do want the expensive eye cream or the new tile in the kitchen, but that for now, I am prioritizing my focus elsewhere. And that gets to be okay.

I had a client who was rocking the free world in her new business. She had begun to stand in her strength in ways that she had not tapped into for a very long time. She left a toxic environment, working for a large bureaucracy, to defining her *own* rules as she attracted her *own* clientele in a business of her *own*.

However, she was mad at herself for not being able to lose the twenty or so pounds that she had slowly put on during her time of working in a stressful environment. I reminded her that her focus was crystal clear at the moment and she was very busy changing a large part of her life, her career and business, for the better. She simply was not prioritizing her weight loss in a way that she could do later when the rate of change slowed for her around work. I asked her to let the guilt go and know that the time would come for her to lose weight when it was right. She was perfectly capable of doing it when she had the time, energy and focus for it.

I recently met with her after she had been on her new work path for over a year. She is now achieving the level of success in her career that she set out for. She has a healthy waiting list of clients, free time with her family, and a beautiful new space filled with positive energy. To top all that off, she is over twenty pounds down, looking lean and healthy.

She told me that I was right. She was able to lose the weight because the time was right to do so. She achieved a level of success with her business that allowed her to include other projects in her life and joined a badass Krav Maga class for women. Not only does she look lovely, but she can now kick your ass too.

The third idea that becomes helpful to remind yourself of when you are tempted to adopt a purchase or behavior of someone else, because you feel it might lead you down a path of success despite your inner guidance system saying that you do not need it, is that this usually only happens when you are not feeling your best. It is quite like the canary in the coal mine who sadly dies when the air quality becomes toxic. When you begin to judge yourself, and feel like you are not enough without a particular thing or behavior, it is often an indicator that you are not currently connected to your true self. Your loving guidance system is on the fritz and it is necessary to reconnect with who you really are and what you are all about.

I will give you some exercises in how to do this later, but for now, write down your ideas of what success means to you. Know that when you are tempted by another's definition of success you become, like the canary, an indicator species for your own well-being.

Sadly, some people live their whole lives in this mediocre state of succumbing to the "should's." "I *should* look different." "I *should* have a remodeled kitchen." They chase and claw their way toward a lifestyle that is defined by others as successful without ever checking in to learn if their own definition of success jives with what they have adopted by their parents or their culture or even their neighborhood.

Take the time now to write your thoughts about success in your journal. Include the *feelings* that you have when you think of your ideas of success and the potential pitfalls mentioned above that you may face. If any of them make you feel anxious or guilty in any way, reconsider that they perhaps are not meant for you. Maybe they are not for you at this stage of your growth and understanding. We all change throughout our lives and our goals and definitions of success need to change with us. If we are operating off of old programming of what success means to us, maybe those that we have inherited by our birth families, but we are maturing in a way that puts us in a far different category of values, we are better off evaluating this discrepancy instead of continuing down a path that will ultimately lead us to feelings of frustration, anger, or worse, apathy.

As I mentioned earlier, clarity is one of the most powerful tools we have at our disposal. Please do not brush this off thinking that you intuitively know what success means to you. I have clients, who, when pressed to do this exercise, find that the writing of their own definitions of success allowed them to almost physically purge the ones that do not really fit them. I see people surprise themselves by what comes out during the writing process.

Be careful of allowing your unique definitions of success to be another area of your life that contributes to self-sabotage by not doing the exercise that could potentially reveal something new.

Congratulations on your resolve to finish this program. Your commitment to yourself is valuable, and I applaud you for your tenacity.

Chapter 11

The Neon Signs

Always bear in mind that your own resolution to succeed is more important than any other.

~Abraham Lincoln – Lawyer, Politician, Equality Seeker

Hopefully you are more clear now about what, exactly, success means to you. I cannot stress enough how important it is to define this clearly.

But a word of warning: Success does not always mean winning. Just because you become crystal clear on what your goals are, and what success is for you, does not mean that life will always go your way. Even with the tools I am going to share with you in a moment, it is helpful to keep in mind that when you conjure up an idea for yourself, you are mostly drawing on the 4% of your conscious brain to do so. I want to help you open up the other 96% of your subconscious brain *and* I want you to think about what the Universe does on your behalf. Remember, we are going to approach this from the scientific point of view as well as the woo-woo one. Embrace it all, friends. Here we go!

Business coach, Jim Rohn, said that *"success is something that you attract by the person that you become."* I really love this because it implies that achieving success is not a passive activity. Remember, we will not be sitting on our couch with a tub of bon-bons thinking positively and expecting our goals to simply manifest themselves. We will be working toward becoming a new version of ourselves as we actively rewire our brains and match our thoughts to the frequency of what we want.

There is a tricky part of this journey that comes up when we have to say goodbye to our former selves. It is important to shed the version of us that no longer supports us in our pursuit of new success. We have to be prepared for the aftershocks this causes, not only for us but for those around us.

When we embark on a journey to grow ourselves we will most certainly cause an effect on the people around us. In fact, I have found that when we become heightened versions of ourselves, entering into the arena where the magic happens, the people who circle our sphere of influence usually react in one of three ways:

One. They are positively affected by your new and improved energy and love how it makes them feel. They ask you how you did it and they embark on their own wild journey into improving their own, unique selves so that they can join you in this new arena. The people who do this with you often become or remain lifelong friends.

Two. They bless and release you on to the arena where the magic happens knowing that change is not right for them at this time. They are genuinely happy for you and wish you well.

They are okay that differences between the two of you are becoming more pronounced as they choose to stay in the arena of safety, comfort and predictability.

Three. They are pissed off. How could you go and do this without them? Now that you are shining so bright with your new-found majesty, they use it as an excuse to compare it against their own dimly lit light source. They often lash out and attempt to share with you all the horrendous scenarios of failure that they can conjure up to try to keep you from staying expansive. You must ward yourself from the negative energy they emit as they try to dominate you with their own low vibrational frequency.

I can say with certainty that some of you who read this will recognize that your relationships with the third group of people have been holding you back. Some of you may have flirted with the opportunity of growing expansively. Maybe you have even vacationed up in the arena where the magic happens, but you continually drop down to previous levels of comfort and predictability when these people, who are afraid of your success, try to tether you there.

This level of "friendly sabotage" shows up in many ways and sometimes is not obvious that it has anything to do with your negative results. But over time, and after hearing many versions of negativity from people you love, your brain will adopt these worries and fears as justifiable reasons not to try anything new. Maybe you have heard one of these scenarios:

"Most businesses fail within the first year. Are you sure you're the one to who will make it work?"

"How could you give up a steady paycheck when you don't know for certain that you'll be able to make as much?"

"Your art is just a hobby, what will you do for *real* work?"

"What if she says no when you ask her out?"

"That's going to take *a lot* of work. Are you sure you're up for it?"

All of these comments seem to be coming from a place of love and caring. But they also put you in a position where you must defend your desires. This in turn, will make you re-think your decision. Perhaps that is their intention, perhaps not, but all of these scenarios are born from a place of fear. They reflect the hesitancy of the person asking the question as they think about how *they* would feel if they were to step out beyond their own comfort zone. Their reaction to your changes is more about their own abilities than about you. In fact, this is one of those Universal truths to hang on to. Reactions are almost always about the person having them, rather than the impetus they are reacting to.

So, what is a person to do when confronted with the Negative Nellies?

In these instances, it is important to intentionally stand in your strength and remember *why* you made the decision to change your life in the first place. Without this strong connection to your purpose you will be easily swayed and persuaded to stay small.

When you are inspired on a daily basis to work toward being your best self, reactions from other people will not mean as much. You can work independently from the opinions of others. Doesn't that sound refreshing?

However, I know that there are some people in our lives who will continue to bring you down, no matter what. For whatever reason, they stubbornly get stuck in the negative position and refuse to budge beyond it. In these instances, it becomes very important that we remember, we cannot change other people without their consent.

There really are only two things that you can do when negative people try to sway you. You can either change your reaction to them or change your proximity to them. Those are the things that you *do* have control over.

As far as you go, remember that some reactions, continually repeated over time, become habits. If you want to grow your outcomes, it is necessary to inventory your reactions to the people around you. Do you become triggered by a sentiment such as the ones listed above? Or do you brush them off like water off a duck's back? Please remember that it is entirely your *choice* what you will do when someone challenges your decisions.

As for the proximity clause, sometimes this simply means that you move to another room while the storm is blowing. Other times the negativity that emanates off of a particular individual will be so strong that you begin to realize that the adjacent room won't be far enough.

It is a sad occurrence when growing ourselves means that we have to trim away friendships, relationships, or even spouses. But if we want to commit to lasting change, the consideration of it needs to be on the table.

There was a time in my life when I became tired of my mediocre outcomes. I knew I needed to be masterful over the way I approached change in my life and it meant that I had to take full stock of the relationships I had collected along the way.

I began to look at each of the relationships in my life through the filter of whether or not this particular relationship buoyed me in some way or dragged me down. I was interested in feeling lifted and supported in my friendships and to be inspired to do the same for them. Instead, I found that I had collected many friends who asked a lot of my time and energy, but did not offer positive energy in return. They were not champions of mine. In fact, I realized that in some sick and twisted form of self-sabotage, I had actually attracted a few people who had a real knack for making me feel like shit - all done under the guise of friendship.

This story takes an interesting turn though.

After doing a lot of painful culling in my friendships, I still found myself experiencing a bit of ennui. I trudged through my days looking at my tasks with the eyes of someone completing chores instead of eyes lit by desire from within. I did not laugh much, and I certainly was not enjoying my life. How could I ask other people to get out of their own way when I was still clearly in my own?

My remedy to this mediocrity began when I tasked myself with becoming my own client. I wondered what I would tell someone else to do in this situation. When I shifted to this perspective, I immediately said to myself, "You *must* gain clarity on exactly what you want."

I sat down that day with a blank sheet of paper and I wrote down four things that I knew I needed to attract into my life to feel happier and more productive.

1) I needed to laugh again. I recognized that I simply was not having much fun in my life and I remembered times of joy and happiness that made me wistful and wanting to recapture the fun.

2) I needed to find a new tribe of women who would empower me and champion me for who I am. I wanted them to be strong enough themselves to not need my company, but rather to want it.

3) I needed to learn something new. I have done ample research in the psychology of happiness and one of the things I have taken to heart is continually to be growing by learning new and interesting things. Taking on new challenges, while at times frustrating during the learning process, paradoxically leads to greater levels of happiness and joy. I wanted that!

4) I needed to exercise more. I had become more sedentary than I had been in the past, and I knew that I was always happier when I moved my body. However, I also knew enough about myself to appreciate the need to be motivated to exercise through an activity that I really enjoyed. I have never been one to want to go to the gym just for a workout, so it needed to be something that I could get really fired up about.

I found tremendous satisfaction in writing this down because once I had clarity about what I was looking for, I knew I would recognize it when I showed up for me.

The *very next day*, I was driving around town and I stopped at a red light behind a car with a decal on the back window that read, "High Altitude Roller Derby, Our Girls Hit H.A.R.D."

I immediately thought to myself, "Ha. I bet those girls have fun!"

The day after that, a Friday evening, I was picking my boys up from after-care at their school when I saw a preschool teacher walking to her car that happened to have a similar roller derby sticker in the window. So, I asked her in the most passive way possible, "If someone thought that they wanted to maybe, possibly, someday think about learning more about roller derby, what would they do?"

She replied excitedly with a gleam in her eyes. "You have to *show up tomorrow* to a warehouse 9 miles out of town for

Skate Skills Weekend. It'll be the only time this year that they take on Fresh Meat! I'll text you the address."

Well, wasn't that interesting. I had written down on a piece of paper, a list of things I was looking for and here, almost immediately, was a big neon sign pointing me toward something that I had never before in my life considered.

That night I cobbled together a pair of skates that a friend of mine had found at the Goodwill, a helmet and wrist guards from my son, knee pads from a neighbor, and elbow pads from the skater-dude-kid down the street. I felt crazy but excited. I was 42 years old and preparing to show up to do something with women who were probably half my age. Add to that the fact that I had not been on roller skates in over 30 years.

Roller skating was my life when I was nine and I regularly skated across the street to my friend, Betsy's house, but that was a lifetime ago and I had no idea if I could still do it.

With a trembling ego and nothing to lose, I walked into a nondescript industrial warehouse in a suburb of Flagstaff. The only remarkable feature to the place was a festive ladybug Mylar balloon and rainbow ribbons tied to the mailbox at the side of the highway indicating that something different was happening inside. Was it ever!

My first introduction to all things roller derby, the introduction that put my fears and inhibitions at bay, was a stunningly gorgeous, tall, athletic woman in her late forties wearing a sparkly silver skirt who said, "Hi! I'm Fifi Sledgehammer. Welcome to roller derby!" I was hooked.

I spent the next two days working my ass off athletically with a huge grin on my face the entire time. I actually giggled. Constantly. I had a lot to learn, but there were amazing women there to help me along the way. There was no shaming or tearing each other down. There was only encouragement and empowerment. There was no turning back for me.

Driving home after the second day, I was struck by how fast the Universe worked to bring me all four components on my wish list in one fell swoop. I had spent two days laughing my butt off, found many new, strong and empowering women who inspired me, I was certainly learning something new and different and was sweaty and tired after two days of rigorous exercise. I attracted everything on my list.

I had to work for them. I had to recognize the signs that I was meant to take action, and then overcome internal barriers that tried to keep me safe and comfortable. But ultimately, I was richly rewarded for having taken action.

After four years, I still skate on my derby team and in fact, just returned two weeks ago, from State Champs. I am not the best on the team, but I work hard at learning new moves and still laugh on a regular basis. I have met the most amazing women playing this sport who are strong and empowered, from all walks of life, and champion me both on and off the track. I am eager to join in grueling workouts several times a week because I know I am working toward something great. Truly, roller derby became the answer to what I was looking for.

I tell you this story, not just because it was the venue for finding beautiful new friendships, but it is a prime example of how quickly the Universe can work in your favor when you gain clarity and write down what you really want - especially when you follow the neon signs.

Have you visited your list of desires in your journal today? Is it possible that the Universe has been sending you bright, neon signs pointing you in an unexpected direction? Be open to the idea that the answer to your dreams may show up in the most unlikely of ways- as roller derby did for me. If you have questions about whether or not something in your life is nudging you in a particular direction, write them down. Let your brain play with the questions and trust your inner guidance system. Know that you may be feeling resistance to a particular activity or person based on your brain trying to keep you safe. Eventually, you will learn to know the difference between the self-sabotaging version of you and the intuitive version of you when you tune into these questions on a regular basis.

Chapter 12

Be Still

The most beautiful thing we can experience is the mysterious; it is the source of all true art and science.

~Albert Einstein – Scientist, Herder of the Mysterious

My clients tease me as I go through exercises with them. I will sometimes excitedly say, "This! This is the most important exercise to do!" But they have heard me say it before. I'm afraid it's true. I really do that. I get all fired up about the impact and change that can come from any one of the things that are meant to rewire our brains for success and positivity.

But this! This is the most important exercise to do. Really.

Actually, it is the combination of the next three concepts where the rubber really meets the road in terms of building a super-highway toward your dreams. We will start with the basics.

But before we do, I want to acknowledge that this is one of the more difficult exercises for some of my clients to adopt.

Our culture has given us all kinds of baggage about this next topic that sometimes stops people in their tracks. Naturally, I would like to remind you of your commitment to yourself as any hidden barriers try to keep you from achieving what is possible.

The grand-master component of change that I am referring to is *meditation*.

Believe me, I understand the reaction some of you are giving me. History has shown me that about half of you are resounding an exuberant "Heck Yeah!", having witnessed firsthand the powerful benefits from meditating. The other half are saying something along the lines of, "Nope. I've tried and I just can't get my mind to quiet down."

For those of you who, for whatever reason, may be reluctant to embrace this as part of your success program, I am here to tell you that it is time to get over your limiting beliefs about why you cannot or will not adopt meditation into your lifestyle. Ironically, the way to get over those limiting beliefs, really, is to sit in meditative silence on a regular basis.

Let's begin with a quick understanding of what I mean when I am talking about using meditation to change the wiring in your brain.

Your brain operates on certain frequencies called brainwaves. The length of the waves determines the particular state of your brain, and different brain waves correspond to different activities in the brain. We will discuss five of them here.

To begin with, most of you right now, assuming that you are still paying attention and have not "zoned out" on me, are operating in the Beta brainwave frequency. In your normal, waking and conscious thinking moments, your brain is operating at Beta. You are in this state when you are thinking critically, and using reason. It is the frequency of high demand, and it is the one that most adults operate in during our work-a-day-worlds.

Unfortunately for us, there are many biochemical responses that are triggered during times of stress, while in our conscious brain, that begin an avalanche of negative physical effects on our bodies. Over time, and if left to continue, these effects can lead to disease and depression.

The next three levels, however, are the antidote to the negative effects of Beta. In fact, they provide the entrance to the playground where neuroplasticity thrives - our subconscious brains. In other words, it is in the next three levels: Alpha, Theta, and Delta, where change and an escape from your limiting beliefs occurs. It is here where we will write the code of new beliefs into your brain.

For beginners, and for our purposes, I will focus heavily on the Alpha state. When we are in Alpha, we have greater access to creativity, learning, intuition, and happiness. It is the "zoned out" state that I mentioned above, and it happens when we are deeply relaxed and are just about to fall asleep or are just waking up.

As it is the entrance to your subconscious mind, it is where I will direct you to do the work to build a new network of beliefs. It is the easiest state to work within for beginner meditators and it works easily and effectively for rewiring our brains.

If you are experienced at meditating, you may find yourself in Theta, the state of extra deep relaxation or even REM sleep. Things that we have learned that are stored in our short-term memory may be transferred to our long-term memory in Theta and it is an extremely valuable brainwave for health and healing.

Delta are the waves of deep, dreamless sleep. Many monks and other life-long meditators are said to be able to affect real, and spectacular change during Delta, but there is no pressure from me to become an expert. It is in Delta where people talk about experiencing collective consciousness and tapping into the infinite knowing of all things. Sadly, it is the description of this kind of emptiness and detachment meditation that I believe scares people off of meditation altogether. I think that people become enamored with tales of beauty found during moments of completely emptying the mind and then they give up on meditating, not knowing that simple deep relaxation is enough to get them going in the right direction.

Moving on, we have the newly discovered Gamma waves. While not much is known about them, we do understand that these waves are different in that they are the fastest frequency: faster than Beta. At this time, scientists disagree about what is going on in our brains during Gamma.

Let's go back now to the Alpha frequency, where we will be experimenting, and do some real problem-solving about how to get into Alpha without tripping over perceived barriers to success.

I would like you to think right now about times in your life when you do "zone out." Do you ever drive home after a long day at work and pull into your driveway only to realize that you were meant to do an errand first? You were running entirely on "autopilot" and you may not even remember making the decision to drive home or not. Interestingly, this all happened while you were in the Alpha frequency.

When we first learn to drive, there are so many rules to follow and pay attention to that we operate in true-form, engaged Beta. But after many years of perfecting the skills involved, our conscious minds check out, given over to our subconscious, and we preform the ritual without having to "think" about what we are doing. This is us entering the Alpha brainwave and it is here where wiring beliefs into your brain becomes easy.

This is both a blessing and a curse. It is a blessing because we can purposefully design a program with our conscious brains to hard-wire in new beliefs that actually support what we are trying to do instead of sabotage us.

It is a curse, because when we are unaware, we sometimes give hidden beliefs a full-access pass to our programming when we are not paying attention.

Take our driving example again. What would happen if, while on your way home from your long, tiring day of work, you should happen to have the news on the radio. What If you were to slip into the Alpha brainwave pattern, which you would be likely to do as you have driven this route a zillion times and you are already tired, while a news story comes on discussing the woes of the present economy? Like it or not, you are more likely to hard-wire a belief into your brain that correlates the terrible economy to than if you hadn't "let" those messages in.

But going back to the blessing side of the Alpha state, if we were to *purposefully* enter an Alpha brainwave state and then feed our brains with positive messaging, they would be more likely to become hard-wired as a new belief into the depths of your brain.

Remember, when you have a belief anchor itself into your brain, you will be compelled to behave in such a way that attempts to prove that belief true. You will be driven to provide yourself with evidence that such a belief holds true, whether it is positive and serves your dreams or negative and leads you to self-sabotage.

Do you want your hard-wired belief to be that the economy sucks and that no one can possibly make it work no matter how hard they try? Or do you want to imprint beliefs that serve your purpose and your direction toward growth and success? Your awareness of when you submit to the Alpha state can keep you from this level of self-sabotage.

I want you to think now about when in your life you slip into the Alpha brainwave on accident. Do a quick inventory of what kinds of information your brain has access to without your knowing. Your subconscious is like a little kid getting away with something his mother would *never* let him do when she's paying attention. It does not always pay attention to the rules. So, use your conscious brain now, in the Beta state, to create stop-gaps for when this is likely to happen.

I would like to demystify the art of beginning meditation a little more for you. Let's go back to what I said about the Alpha brainwave state. It is something that you are likely very familiar with, but perhaps have never done it on purpose. I will be asking you to do just that, so here are some tricks of the trade to get you into Alpha without too much trouble.

First of all, it might be best for those of you who have an internal blockage of some sort aimed at meditation to begin thinking of this simply as relaxation exercises, because truly, they are one and the same.

Second, it is probably wise to rid yourself of any preconceived notions about *how* you must meditate. You do not need to sit in any complicated position. You do not even have to have your eyes closed, though for starting out I recommend it to eliminate distractions.

Simply make yourself comfortable. If you would rather lie down than sit comfortably, that's okay as long as you do not tend to drift off to sleep. And even then, if you want to meditate for the purpose of helping yourself fall asleep, then go for it. It is important to remember to keep yourself from getting caught up in any preconceived rules.

For now, simply take a few minutes to do the following things:

Close your eyes and make yourself comfortable.

Breathe slowly and deeply into your belly. Breathing through your nose is best, but again, if allergies or other sinus issues keep you from doing this, do not let it be an excuse to get out of trying to meditate.

Focus momentarily on relaxing each part of your body. Begin with the top of your head, then go to your forehead, your eyes, your face, your jaw and then your neck. Focus on relaxing each part of your body all the way down to your feet. All the while, keep breathing slowly and deeply.

Move your focus to a new body part with each inhale and relax it with each exhale.

If you find your mind wandering off simply guide it gently back to whatever you were focusing on before you started meandering. Try not to judge yourself or berate your efforts. Simply find a new area of your body to focus on and keep going.

And that is it - SERIOUSLY. It need not be any more complicated than that.

Try this now and see if you feel your body sink into a deeper state of relaxation. Bring your focus to how it really feels. I am very serious. Put this book down and take the three minutes for yourself that this exercise takes.

If this body scan exercise didn't work for you, and you did not feel your body sink into a deep relaxation, it's okay. They do not call it a meditation *practice* for nothing. It really does get easier over time. Quite frankly, this was too difficult for me when I started this routine in my life, so I got help in the form of guided meditation and I highly recommend it for anyone starting out. Yes, it is important to know how to relax your own body without the help of some external force, but sometimes, paying attention to another voice that tells you what to do is easier than trying to regulate your own voice in your head.

Luckily, we live in an age where guided meditation is available everywhere. You no longer need to visit a new age crystal store to buy a tape or CD that can only be found among the esoteric. Nowadays, you can simply download an app onto your phone and listen wherever you go. Do a quick search for "guided meditation" or "relaxation exercises" on your phone, tablet or computer and you will come up with thousands of free examples at your fingertips.

Here is what's even better about doing this. Remember how I said that in the Alpha state we have access to our subconscious brains in a way that makes it easy to rewire our thought patterns? We simply need to feed our listening brain with new beliefs that support rather than decrease our successes.

Guided meditation takes advantage of this in the best possible way. When you search for available meditations you will find those that not only help you relax into an Alpha (or perhaps even Theta) state, but that also feed your brain with positive, empowering messaging. You simply need to commit to the process, relax, and let your brain swim in the gorgeousness of positivity and growth. How fantastic is that? And yet, so many people who know about this, do not meditate on a regular basis.

But you will. Add this phrase now to your journal: *I commit to feeding my brain with positive messaging every day while in a deeply relaxed state.*

What happened to your body when you relaxed just now? There are too many benefits of meditating to list here, but I will share a few so that you know why captains of industry and leaders of nearly every domain are committed to meditation as a daily practice.

When you breathe deeply you lower your respiratory rate, increase your blood flow and lower your heart rate. Your immune response kicks in and inflammation decreases. Your muscles relax, pain responses decrease and energy increases. In your brain, serotonin levels increase naturally, influencing your mood. Your emotions become easier to regulate and information organizes itself. Feelings of brain fog decrease as your learning ability and your memory improve.

For our purposes, we will be using a daily meditation habit to overwrite new, positive beliefs onto our old outdated limiting ones. All the other benefits are icing on the cake. And hopefully, once you start you will see the benefits stacking up and you will never think about stopping.

Chapter 13

The Language of Success

Science does not know its debt to imagination.

~Ralph Waldo Emerson – American Transcendentalist Poet

The larger field of anthropology contains four subfields: Sociocultural, or sometimes simply called cultural anthropology, the study of cultures, both past and present; Archeology, the study of cultural artifacts; Physical Anthropology, the study of human remains; and Linguistics, the study of language and the impact it has on cultures as well as the impact that culture has on languages.

Within the subfield of linguistics, we learn that language, syntax and word meanings change over time, even within a singular culture or subculture. Through time, a certain word may take on several different meanings or morph with the mood of the culture.

Take the word *dope* for instance. When I say the word dope, even among people within my own demographic, many different meanings will arise; and not all will be original homonyms of the word.

Some of you will think that I am speaking of someone who is dumb, stupid, or maybe ignorant. Some will assume I am talking about drugs or weed (another word that has taken on multiple meanings over time) and yet others among the more hip crowd will think that I am describing something spectacular.

My point is, that over time, words can collect a patina of meaning that changes with usage. Sometimes, this occurs even within families who adopt a word or phrase that means something entirely different than what mainstream culture believes it to mean because of a particular story or colorful character. My own family of origin invented several examples of this.

Thanks to the elder males of the Merkel family, especially my beloved, departed Uncle Arl, we have an entire dictionary of words that are uncommonly used. For instance, *olived* means made a mistake; as in, "I just olived the recipe for this dish and it turned out terrible." *Farb* means to make something up, as in, "I farbed your details to her so that she might be interested in you." And *stobbs* are either steaks or golf clubs and used like, "Let's run to the store and pick up a couple of stobbs for the grill."

If someone were to use one of these words or even something that sounded like it came from the Merkel dictionary, I would likely burst out laughing even if it were meant in more somber use. For me, my subculture has changed the way I use language and therefore the effects it has on my brain.

I bring this up here because if we are going to use language to *tell* our subconscious brain how we want it to rewire, we need to be very careful about the language we use. We do not want to fall into a trap because of multiple or alternate meanings confusing our direction.

That is why I now want to share with you the language of the subconscious mind. Because if we can communicate with our subconscious in its own language, we can bypass any unforeseen complications of *oliving* our success.

The language of the subconscious mind is *pictures*. And the way to speak to it is through *visualization*.

We will be using visualization, coupled with meditation to tell your subconscious brain what success looks like to us.

Remember when I talked about the fact that the subconscious brain needs to filter a tremendous amount of information at any given time through your beliefs, and send only what is important to you on to your conscious brain? In order to filter that much information your brain has to use heuristics in order to get all of that work done in one fifth of a second.

We are going to take advantage of the constant work that your subconscious brain does by using visualization. In other words, we are going to use our conscious brains to devise a plan to trick your subconscious brain into believing that something you want in your success journey *has already come true*.

You see, your subconscious is working so fast that it really does not know the difference between something that you visualize is happening or something that is really happening. Both scenarios, to your brain, are true.

Did you know that if I were to use a functional brain scan of your brain to see which muscles fired as you sliced an apple in half, certain areas of your brain would light up in accordance to the thought processes and muscles used? Then, if I were to use the same functional brain scan while you relaxed your body and mind, and then visualized yourself cutting the apple in half, the same exact areas of your brain would light up in accordance to the thought processes and muscles used.

We truly can trick your brain into thinking that something you visualize, even if it has never happened before, is true. And remember, your brain is always looking for evidence that the beliefs it holds are true, and looks for that evidence in your behaviors. If your brain does not know the difference between behaviors that are true in reality, versus evidence that is true in your made-up visualizations, you can bypass time and effort in the re-wiring process by providing evidence before the success has even shown up for you.

If your brain believes in the reality of a successful outcome during a certain situation it will compel you to behave in accordance to that belief. Furthermore, it will change the filters to highlight the opportunities and possibilities in your surroundings to make sure that you can capitalize on these beliefs in the best possible way.

I am sure you have heard of the most decorated Olympian of all time, Michael Phelps, who rings in at a whopping 28 medals. You may have seen him with his earbuds in before a race kind of "zoning out." This is Michael visualizing the race to come. Since he was young, his coach always reminded him to "play his tapes" which meant to visualize each and every stroke of his winning races. Before Michael ever hits the water in any given race his brain believes that he has already won the race on a regular basis. His body is then compelled to do the same. Winning is literally an everyday occurrence for him because he visualizes himself winning every day.

But this little trick is not limited to Olympic athletes. I also have used this technique to great effect. Sometimes it is almost eerie how well it works.

Years ago, when I decided that I wanted to throw my hat in the ring to apply for the position of CEO of a well-known youth non-profit in my town, I decided that if I was going to go for it, then I was going to do it right. Handing in my application became a secondary preparation to all the visualization I did to *see* myself in the position.

During the application process, I spent time each and every day visualizing as many aspects of the position that I could think of. I imagined which route I would take to drive to work, how my office would look, what I would wear, and what type of people I would talk with throughout the day.

After a successful first round of interviews, their choice was narrowed down to me and one other candidate. They told me that in addition to interviewing with the existing CEO and staff separately, I was to make a presentation to their (rather large) Board of Directors about my vision for the organization.

In addition to the extensive preparation I made in developing a top-notch presentation, I kicked my visualization into high gear.

While I knew what the conference room where my presentation would be held looked like, every other aspect of what was to come was pure fiction.Therefore, I visualized the reactions of the board during and after my presentation being not just complementary, but enthusiastically in my favor. I figured that if I visualized a truly over the top reaction, even if I came close, I would win the day.

You know the saying. "Shoot for the moon, even if you miss you'll land among the stars." That was my theme.

With this in mind, I decided that the most over the top thing that could happen was that they gave me a standing ovation. Now, I know that a board of directors of *any* organization is not going to show their hand during a job interview in such a way, but it was a means toward visualizing success that provided me with true, physical evidence of my achievement without trying to interpret people's smiles or nods. I made visualizing easy on myself by feeding my brain with a simple to see, positive outcome.

There was my visualization, for an entire week, playing through my brain on a perpetual loop. I would rock my presentation, and they would be so overwhelmed with my abilities that they would stand up and clap. Anywhere I had quiet time during the interim week between my first and second interviews, this scene played in my head. While I was in line at the grocery store, driving my car, just waking up or going to sleep, this loop was playing through my head.

The evening finally came for me to share my ideas with the board of this great organization, and two things happened that rocked my world and changed the way I think about visualization forever.

The first is that I arrived for the presentation *knowing* that I was going to rock it. I truly surprised myself by my lack of nerves that I had assumed would be my constant companion throughout the evening. Because I had seen myself rocking the presentation dozens of times, my brain was convinced that this time would not be any different. My visualization had fundamentally changed my level of confidence going in by negating the launch of the biochemical soup of stress hormones that otherwise would have been deployed. I held my head high and vibrated on the frequency of success throughout, feeling cool as a cucumber.

The second thing that happened that evening is something of tall tales and fantasy. I was able to deliver one of the most perfect talks in my lifetime. I felt in the zone the entire time, playing off the energy in the room as if it were a finely tuned instrument. I lost time and had fun. Then, when I finished, I had created such a crescendo of excitement, that the entire room leapt to their feet and gave me, you guessed it - a standing ovation.

I could not believe it. I almost wept in joy from the absurdity of it all. I mean, who reveals their cards that way in a job interview? In my visualization, I purposefully went beyond what I thought might be possible so that I did not undershoot. But this. This was incredible. It was *exactly* as I imagined it.

From then on, I never questioned the power of visualization again. With clarity of what you want comes the ability to *imagine* what you want. When you can tell your brain using its own language, you can change its filters so that you are compelled to do everything in your power to make it so.

Another piece that makes this work is the part that I cannot fully explain. I feel as if the Universe organizes itself around what you want when you become crystal clear about it. This is the woo-woo side of things that exists either entirely in a spiritual place or in the quantum realm with an understanding that I have not yet obtained. Either way, I know that the Universe is on my side and has my back when I am clearly visualizing what I want.

I was blessed with an active imagination as a young child. Sadly, I was often told to get my head out of the clouds and to stop being so overly dramatic. I was teased about my wild fantasies of what was possible when I was little and for a time, as I aged, my rich inner imagination clouded.

In recent years, I have worked hard to reclaim the power of imagination because I now know its benefits when I employ visualization for inviting what I want into my life.

> *"Imagination is everything. It is the preview of life's coming attractions. Imagination is more important than knowledge"*
> *~Albert Einstein*

Why is Einstein so lauded for his knowledge but not his imagination? We grow up in an education system that teaches us to learn *things*- not to enhance our dreamy nature. In fact, we have even created systems and institutions that prohibit the use of creative imagination in the world of problem solving.

Let me be your champion to help you bring it back. Wherever you are with your imagination skills, take this as an invitation to cultivate the process and grow the craft. The more wild and crazy you become, as we have seen, the more richly rewarded you may be. Paint bright, full, and beautiful pictures in your mind of what is to come in your life when you reach your goals and do not be afraid to invent a little more along the way.

Chapter 14

An Emotional Boost

You are beautiful because you let yourself feel, and that is a brave thing indeed.

~Shinji Moon – Poet, Author of The Anatomy of Being

We now know that meditating or relaxing into the Alpha state allows us to fundamentally change the programming in our subconscious minds. If we want to do so, we can use the language of the subconscious, that is visualization, to imprint new beliefs and ways of seeing success onto our brains.

There is a third technique, that when combined with meditation and visualization creates the grand trifecta of change and inviting success into your life.

Do you remember when I discussed early brain research that told us that 80% of the decision-making process was filtered through our emotions? And that our intentions were sometimes hijacked by our emotions taking over what otherwise would have been a rational decision?

Here, we are going to analyze the use of our emotions again. But this time we will do some reverse engineering of the process, creating a scenario where we hijack our outcomes for the better- on purpose.

Back in my days of working on epidemiological projects as a medical anthropologist, we studied much about stages of change theories among many medical belief models. These theories describe how, in attempts to change our behavior, we move through many different stages of contemplating change before we actually take the leap. In general, we must contemplate our proximity to a threat or a benefit *seven* times before we consider that the given change is worthwhile.

For instance, if I were to build an anti-smoking campaign I would do so in a way that allows you, as the consumer of my campaign, to learn about the threats of smoking seven different times, on average, before I would expect that you might change your smoking habits. I would need to deliver multiple awareness and education modalities for your exposure. Then, I would need to make sure that they were consistent enough for you to tie them together so that the message built upon itself instead of seeming like seven different messages.

For those of you in sales, this may seem somewhat familiar as the sales theories of seven. In fact, they are exactly the same. For anyone in sales, it is conventional wisdom that you "touch" your prospect about seven times before attempting to close the sale. That is, your client must hear a radio ad, see a brochure, meet a person in the industry, visit a showroom, hear a testimonial, collect a business card and see a logo on a billboard, before thinking to herself, "hmm, I wonder if I could use that product or service to help solve my problem."

In consulting in the non-profit sector, I use these theories with great success. It is not wise to ask someone for money before going through a relationship cultivation process. That process needs to allow for somewhere in the neighborhood of seven occurrences.

However, there is a way to bypass each of the seven steps of the process. That is by infusing a sufficient amount of emotion into the perceived threat and/or benefit.

If you are able to make your case personal enough to your client or consumer, they will work their way through the stages of change in an instant. When you do so, you allow a signal in the brain to recognize that this is important enough to fast track.

I'll give you an example from my childhood.

When I was in junior high school I was friends with a girl named Laurie, who refused to wear a seatbelt when riding in a car. Her father had told her that she was more likely to die in a car accident by being trapped by her seatbelt than she was to be saved by one. Because of this, they cut all the seatbelts out of their family cars and Laurie was not allowed to wear one in any other cars she rode in.

As you may know, it is an understatement to say that junior high friendships mean the world to a young girl, and I was incredibly emotionally invested in keeping Laurie as a friend. Therefore, in the logic of the 13-year-old teenage girl brain, whose prefrontal cortex would not be fully developed for several more years mind you, I decided that I too, would refuse to wear my seatbelt while riding in a car. I am sure I must have made my parents crazy for several months as I adopted a stance of obstruction toward their logical cries of safety. They must have been in the 'choose your battles' mode and besides, they were not always paying attention anyway.

This madness played out for a while until one day, the sister of another friend of ours crashed her car into a tree. The impact was so severe that it sent Georgia, the sister of our friend, sailing through the front window where she hit her head on a tree and died instantly. I need not tell you that she was NOT wearing a seatbelt.

Upon hearing of my friend's tragic loss, it took me all of about half a second before my brain was convinced that the better plan, when faced with the two options, was to always wear a seatbelt. And of course, I have religiously worn my seatbelt ever since.

You see, my brain was faced with a decision-making process containing both logic and emotion. But the emotion involved with keeping a teenage friendship, however important, was overshadowed by the emotion I felt when my friend tragically lost her sister to a violent, and preventable accident.

My brain allowed me to bypass all the contemplation I would have done in an emotionally neutral environment. I acted immediately. I changed my behavior forever because my beliefs were firmly set. Seatbelts saved lives. They still do. Wear one!

I recognize that in this example, it is a powerfully negative emotion that led to my irrevocable trust in seatbelts. But it could just as easily have been an equally powerful positive emotion with the same result.

I evoke the rules of Disnely/Pixar's *Monsters Inc.* (2001) here. Remember the movie where monsters scared children at night to capture the energy from the children's screams to power their city? They ultimately learned that laughter created a far more powerful energy boost than fear, concluding what we all know, that positivity is better than negativity in every way.

I bring this up because I am going to ask you to manufacture your own positive emotion. Then I am going to ask you to overlay the positive feelings onto your visualization while you are in the Alpha brainwave state. Do you see how this builds?

Do something for me right now. I would like you to write in your journal, five things that make you blissfully happy. It could be a memory of a special day, a person, or a place. Maybe it's a thing that you own that brings you immense joy. Whatever it is for you, write down a comprehensive list. I want it to be a list of things that will raise you to a happy state *without fail*.

For me, all I need to do is think about my two boys peacefully asleep to create a physical buzz in my heart. I can feel a sense of vibration in my chest that corresponds with the love I feel for them when I witness them at rest.

Notice in your body where happiness shows up for you. For some people, it is in their heart center, as with me. For others, I have found that happiness is felt in their faces. It does not matter where it shows up for you. What matters is for you to recognize a *physical* sensation in response to a thought. Once you feel it, you will know what you are looking for when you overlay happiness onto your visualizations. Naturally, I hope that your visualizations of success will make you burst with joy all on their own. But if you are new to this process, you may want to take some time prior to your visualization to drum up the feeling of happiness and joy in whatever way you can.

Incidentally, isn't it a wonderful feeling to know that you can *manufacture* joy whenever you want? It's on demand, like Netflix. Just log on and go. I know that seems like a simple thing, but tuck this trick away in your journal. Keep a bookmark on your list of things that make you happy. You can go back to it any time you need a boost and manufacture joy where there wasn't any a moment ago.

Putting these three tactics together; mediation, visualization and emotion provide you with the foundation of inviting any kind of success into your life that you desire. It seems simple, doesn't it? But perhaps for that reason alone people tend to discount its power.

I believe the difficult part comes in the form of developing clarity about exactly what it is that you want to invite into your life. Spend some time with this. Know that it can change and grow as you do. Your life is not a static document and your dreams need not be either.

Chapter 15

The Battery Pack

No one has ever become poor by giving.

~ Anne Frank – Brave Diarist

If you were to close this book right now with the tools that you already have, you would be well equipped for shaping your brain in a way that facilitates positive change and success. The new neural pathways that you will build through gaining clarity about what you want, meditating on a daily basis, and adding visualization and emotion will organize your life to accept success. Congratulations on getting this far.

I know you have stuck with this powerful journey and are really giving it a go because you told yourself that you would. And I believe in you. Is it simple? Yes. Is it difficult to do? Yes. Is it worthwhile? Yes.

But there is much left in the book that you may be wondering about, and I want to continue with revealing two wildly important components to living a life of success versus inviting it in every once in a while. I call these two components *batteries* because they help to supercharge your efforts to inviting success for the abundant life you are creating.

Right now, I am going to let you in on the secret to what these two batteries to success are. These next two concepts are so life-changing that they fuel any effort you make into convincing yourself and the world around you that change is afoot.

This! This is the exercise for you to pay attention to. I know I have said that before, but in truth, if a client comes to me in crisis, I skip everything else and jump to the batteries first.

I should interject here that not many people do come to me in crisis. I know my limits, and I am not a therapist or counselor. I will always refer out to other professionals someone who needs true therapeutic help. My clients who come to me in "crisis mode" are simply people who have lived for a long time viewing the world through a lens of negativity. They tend to wake up each day wondering how the world is going to screw them today and they are on the lookout for the bad things. For someone who is simply hamstrung by their outlook, I give them these next two exercises.

The first of these two batteries is to spend time each day, without fail, writing down things that you are grateful for. And while you are writing them down, take the time to really *feel* the presence of the emotion. Gratitude, when truly felt, offers you a vibrational frequency similar to happiness. Once again, we are manufacturing our own happiness by changing our thoughts. You will need to have gratitude become a habit if you want for anything significant in your life to change.

The reason why some people do not already practice a high level of gratitude leads us to one of the great paradoxes of attracting success in your life. You see, you cannot bring something bigger or better into your world by hating what you already have. Focusing on the lack of what you have simply brings you more lack.

Let's analyze this concept by using information from the neurosciences. Again, we have to work with the fact that your subconscious brain works fast and furious to filter through gobs of information at any given time using shortcuts get the job done. One of the ways this shows up for us is in how it processes negatives. It doesn't.

Here is how this works. Your brain hears you say to yourself, "I hate being broke. I don't want bills to rule my world anymore, I never want to be broke again!" In order for your brain to process this, it has to make meaning of the things you've said and will do so in a similar fashion to how we diagramed sentences when we were in elementary school. Your brain has to make sense of what being broke means, as well as bills ruling your life and being broke again.

The negating "do not's" do not register in your brain at all. Your brain has something else to focus on now - being broke and bills. It can even create a visual representation of what that means for you. It will not, however, pay any attention to the fact that you mean to tell it *not* to.

I will give you another, perhaps easier, example. Right now, I would like you to NOT think of a green sea turtle. In order for you to make sense of what I am saying at all, you have to think of the green sea turtle first. Then you have to think of something that replaces the green sea turtle. If you are still with me, you may have replaced it with a purple cup or an orange car. But your brain is not likely to stick with you past the first step. It has moved on to other filtering business. Your brain will likely just hang on to the vision of the sea turtle.

If you say this with emotion, whether it is, "I don't want to be broke!" or "I don't want to think of a green sea turtle!", your brain will flag that as important and filter to bring you *more* of it.

What does this have to do with gratitude, you may ask? Well, if you are looking at all the things or situations in your life that you want to improve upon, but are saying that you *don't want* that thing or situation anymore, you may actually be sabotaging your efforts to get an upgrade. The paradox I mentioned above lies in the fact that we absolutely *must* fall in love with the things and situations we have right now if we want any hope to improve upon them. You can begin that process by being relentlessly grateful for every little thing you want an improvement on, no matter how shitty it seems to you now.

Perhaps you have an old, barely-working car that is falling apart in your driveway that you feel a sense of loathing for every time you have to drive it in public. You want something better more than you have wanted anything before. Being deeply grateful for it is your key to improving upon it. From that point, set your clear intention on exactly what you do want, and keep your brain from fixating on the suck surrounding the car you have now. You can ward yourself from bringing more painful and awful things from coming into your life through focusing on the good of what you have versus the bad of what you wish you didn't have.

There is another way that gratitude will improve your success positioning, and this is where science meets woo.

You see, the Universe loves to see you happy. And when you are happy, it wants to bring you more reasons to be happy. This goes along with the theories of vibrational energy endorsed by quantum physicists and new agers alike.

When you are feeling deeply in love with the crappy car in your driveway the Universe has a way of saying, "Dang, that love and gratitude feels good. You know what else would feel good? If he had that fancy-schmancy new ride he's been thinking about, he'd feel even better. Let's arrange for that to happen!"

Ok, so it might not happen exactly like that, but I can tell you from experience that the Universe has a way of arranging itself to create what you want as soon as you make a habit of gratitude for what you have.

Besides, it feels great to start the day thinking about what you love and are grateful for and to end the day the same way. There are many nights when my brain is furiously working out some life-altering problem attempting to keep me awake. I can shut down the spinning rather easily by listing as many things that I can think of to be grateful for.

The things you think about to be grateful for do not need to be huge, resume-style things. Yes, I am grateful for my husband and children every day but I also take the time to notice and love on the smaller things. Today, I spent time being grateful for warm water and the access I have to an abundance of it. I am grateful for my favorite pen that I used earlier today to take some notes. I really love that pen. I am also grateful for the taste and nutrition provided by my lunch. I am grateful for that Stellar Jay that is chirping outside my window right now, and this apple in front of me that started as a blossom and grew on a tree for me to enjoy when I want.

Do you see what I am doing here? Some of you will recognize this as a practice in mindfulness. Mindfulness is a type of meditation that asks you to be fully in the present, here and now. Once again, we are overlaying emotion onto the process of focus and supercharging our outcomes.

Your new, favorite journal is a great place to list your gratitude each day. Try to be consistent about listing five things you are grateful for in the morning and five things again in the evening before you go to bed. You will be glad for both beginning and ending your day in a framework of gratitude.

Alas, this particular success toy takes two batteries, and I have only given you one: Gratitude. The next way to power up your success supercharger is through generosity.

Yes, giving is one of the most powerful ways of receiving what you want. Like its sister, gratitude, generosity is a powerful paradox. I know how Westerners dislike paradox, but I will ask you again to embrace it.

Giving creates an aspect of flow in your life like no other. In truth, I really have no neuroscience to back up the benefits of giving beyond the sense of how good it makes you feel. I do have ample evidence from my coaching practice that a great sense of spiritual flow is alive and well. Yes, I am knowingly asking you to step fully into the pool of wonder with me here to see if this works for you as well. I am quite sure that it will.

If we use the word abundance broadly, and I think we should, to mean an abundance of everything good, we can agree that everything we seek is abundance, can we not? The presence of abundance in your life is like the flow of water.

If water sits unmoving for too long, it creates a stagnation that becomes host to all sorts of pestilence. One way to correct such a stagnation is to invite the water to flow once again, causing any kind of nastiness that has set in to dissipate through flow.

Abundance in our lives works much the same way. When we hold on to what we have too tightly, problems begin to arise. This is evident in relationships, wealth, and sometimes possessions. But when we pass along our abundance to others, we are greatly rewarded for having done so.

Remember the person who wakes up wondering how the world was going to screw them today? If they were to change that habit, a new routine could change their life. Think about the change that would happen if each day upon waking up, they listed five things they are grateful for, then deliberately wondered what kind of gift they were going to give away today. I know their general attitude and outlook on life *will* change from this routine.

To change your outlook, I ask you to give a gift every day. That is your next exercise. I would like you to give something, anything, to someone each day for the next three weeks. Each day.

It does not need to be a big thing, or even cost you any money, but I would like it to be an unexpected gift that you give on purpose. Document in your journal the gifts that you give each day. When you write them down, sink into how good it feels to have given the gift and imagine how great you made the recipient feel. Again, know that this good feeling brings you closer to what you want and creates a sense of flow in your life.

Resist the temptation to look back on your day and figure that holding the elevator for that nice woman was your gift. While yes, it was done with good intention, and you should definitely keep committing to gestures such as this, it was not a preconceived gift. Therefore, it should not count as your gift of the day.

Also, resist the temptation to go out and buy something each day. Use this as a chance to clear through some things that you no longer use and hand them off to someone who would. While there are many great charities that take donations of used items, it is better to think of an individual who might truly enjoy the particular item. You might say to a coworker, "you know, I really love this scarf and I just never wear it, but I notice that you wear scarves all the time, so I thought of you. I'd like you to have it."

Gifts can also be bought, but can remain small. One of my favorite things to do when I am at a store that has small candies at the register is to buy one and then, as I am leaving, to hand it to the cashier. I say, "I actually bought this one for you. I hope you have a great day." The unexpected nature of this gift from a stranger never fails to brighten someone's day.

These days, I am happy to report, it is not unheard of for someone in a drive-through to pay for the car behind them. I fully support this as well. Just remember, if giving puts you in a financial hole, then the good feeling of the gift will back-fire on you. Make sure that you give within your means.

Other great gifts to give are gifts of time, expertise, and even written gratitude or thank you notes. When was the last time you received a hand written thank you note in the mail? They are so precious these days that they have become like small, wrapped gifts.

Take some time now to make a list in your journal of all the gifts you can think of to give, and who you would like to give gifts to. The intent of this is to create a world where you are constantly looking to be of service to someone. When you view your life through the filter of generosity you will feel fantastic each time you give your gift of the day and you will be able to tap into that fabulous feeling every time you read about each gift you gave in your journal. Over time, your journal will be stocked with many examples of things that create the feeling of happiness and joy - for you!

I believe whole heartedly that when you begin practicing gift giving on a regular basis, you will be surprised by how many gifts you will begin to receive. Out of the blue, people will turn up having thought of you and will bestow you with gifts.

This happened to me quite recently when I revived my own three-week giving practice. I try to give all the time, but I was prompted a few weeks ago to create more flow in my life, so I recommitted to a daily giving schedule as I am asking you to do.

Three days after giving very small gifts I arrived to my office to see a beautiful bouquet of flowers on my desk tied in a gorgeous orange, satin bow. It turned out that in my absence the previous evening, an old friend had stopped by with a random love bomb for me. I had not seen her for ages and she and I, though very friendly, had never shared gifts before. It was so out of the big, blue sky that I had no doubt it was a kiss from the Universe telling me that my faucet of flow was beginning to open again.

The other component of generosity that I cannot neglect to mention is receivership. Many people I speak to in my practice have learned, from our culture, to be unskilled in the receiving department. We are often taught to exercise ample humility and therefore deflect compliments as well as gifts. You know the script, "you shouldn't have" or "oh no, this old thing?" or "no, I'm not pretty, but you. You are!"

Remember, these kinds of remarks, heard over and over again, become clear indicators to your subconscious brain that you should not pay any attention to the nice things that are said about you. Deflecting gifts or compliments is a great way to stop the flow. If the Universe thinks the gift is not well received (yes, I'm anthropomorphizing the Universe again), gifts will cease to arrive.

Practice receiving graciously. If someone gives you a compliment, thank them. Sincerely. And do not try to deflect it back to them. It takes some level of practice, but give it a shot.

Here is a good one to try. The next time someone says "I love you", try not to say, "I love you too" back to them. Try to simply say, "Thank you." See if the world blows up or if you fall into the crocodile pit. My guess is that it will feel super weird, but nothing really terrible will happen. It's okay to tell the person you are exchanging compliments with what you are up to. In fact, it might be nice when you all of a sudden break some unspoken code of conduct to tell them that you are attempting to be a better receiver. Get them in on the game and see if they can do it too. My guess is that we can all use a little help in the receiving end of life.

Implement these two batteries to boost your power of positivity with gusto. I know how important they become in building a lifetime of success.

Welcoming Abundance

Chapter 16

Let Go

We must let go of the life we have planned, so as to accept the one that is waiting for us.

~Joseph Campbell – Mythologist, Chronicler of the Hero's Journey

I've seen it time and time again. Someone does the right things to attract success into their lives only to let it slip through their fingers and they have to start all over again. In fact, I believe this sporadic cycle of abundance and loss is what most people experience in their lives until they become purposeful about their outcomes. They will get really excited about something, attempt to attract it, and then do not know what to do with it when it arrives.

This happens because they do nothing to change their overall lifestyle. Their success set-point stays the same and any supporting beliefs they gain are shadowed out by other means of self-sabotage. Do not let this happen to you.

This next section is about the lifestyle habits you will need to truly welcome your life of success once it arrives. You do not want to snub your nose at the good things you attract once they show up for you. You do not want those good things and experiences to leave you. The remainder of the work left for you to accomplish is about ingraining high standards of success into everything you do. I will point out some common pit-falls that people find themselves in and help you achieve mastery over them. After all, to become a master at any skill does not mean to do it sporadically, it means to do it every time, without fail. In the very least, it means to recognize when you are not being masterful and to know the tools to correct your situation.

Think about who you might be hurting or keeping in the dark by playing small. Being small and not playing up to your potential does not serve you. Nor does it serve the people around you.

A few years ago, a friend of mine who works as a nurse in the hospital told me a story of a co-worker of his. He told me of a woman who had gone to school to become a naturopathic physician. She identified as a healer and she had dreams of opening a practice where she could help people heal in beautiful, natural ways. Sadly though, her attempts to attract enough clients to her business practice failed, and she was faced with needing a job to sustain her. Still being attracted to healing, she became certified as a nurse and secured a job in an allopathic hospital.

While I never met this person, this story made me very sad. Here is someone who, for whatever reason, gave up on her dreams of working in her chosen field. She settled for a system that promoted health in an entirely different way. She did find security, but at what expense?

Reaching and growing is not easy. But when we have dreams for ourselves, I believe that they point to our purpose.

When we overcome obstacles, and follow our dreams we have more of an opportunity to live in alignment with our version of success. I want this for you.

Every time I say yes to myself in ways that require me to push through preconceived barriers, I am richly rewarded. Sometimes I have to do so with great attention to self-care and attention to when my brain is attempting to sabotage my efforts and keep me safe. However, I push through anyway in the faith that growth is essential for me. It leads to my ultimate happiness.

At any given time, we are either growing or declining. Our very dynamic nature suggests that we do not hover in a moment of stasis. I ask you, are you growing? I would venture to say yes, indeed you are. The very fact that you were attracted to this book suggests that you are willing to stretch yourself. If you have completed the exercises thus far, you have made a commitment to yourself to continue to stretch your limits. I congratulate you on that.

But we are not done yet. Let's continue on our journey welcoming the abundance that I believe is your birthright.

~

The first step in committing to mastery is perhaps the most important step of all. Have I said that before? Truly, I do not mean to diminish the importance of this because it really is one of the make-it or break-it exercises in this process. If you fail to do this, you may sabotage all efforts you have put in so far. But if you can embrace yet another paradox, you may be richly rewarded.

You must let go of your attachment to your outcome.

I know, this sounds ridiculous on the heels of me asking you throughout this book to become crystal clear on what you want- even giving you steps to achieve exactly those goals.

Here is the rub. When you concoct your scheme to achieve a particular milestone in your life, you are doing so within the limitations of your own brain. Even if these dreams are inspired from deeply felt beliefs and inspirations borne out of the depths of your larger, subconscious brain, they are still limited. The power of possibility that comes from your conscious is miniscule compared to what the Universe could cook up for you.

When we hold on tightly to our version of exactly what will bring us the feeling of success, we limit the possibilities of achieving exactly that feeling. What if something better came along for you? What if, in some greater-than-you version of the world around you, life organized itself so that you were brought happiness, joy and abundance in a way that you never thought was possible? Would you turn it down?

This is the lesson of *allowing*, and I recognize that it is not always easy to do when you become passionate and committed to a goal. I am not going back on what I said about the importance of setting your goals- your lighthouses. But once these are set, and you are committed to them, you must let go of the necessity that they *alone* will bring you success.

I once knew a woman who liked diamond rings very much and was excited about the possibility of receiving one from a suitor who would hopefully become her fiancé. Her attraction to such rings led her to research exactly what she wanted and she showed pictures to her boyfriend of what she hoped to receive. Being a practical woman, the picture of her 'goal' ring was stunning, but not overly flashy or beyond the financial means of her man. Not that she would not have wanted something larger, she was simply a reasonable woman and understood the meaning of limitations.

Unbeknownst to her, her soon-to-be fiancé had previously received a ring from his family that had been passed down through the generations. It was a larger, higher quality diamond ring in an antique setting, with more family sentiment than anything that he could buy from a store. But he knew his beloved had her heart set on the ring in the picture, indeed, nearly insisted on it, and he was determined to start a marriage in a way that made her happy.

Because of his dedication to her strong desire, he sold his family heirloom to buy her the ring of her dreams. They were both happy, and I will probably never know if she learned about the forsaken heirloom as we have lost touch over the years. But this story always stuck in my mind as a stark example of limiting the possibilities when you direct your desires too specifically.

Allowing takes practice. It is not easy when you dream of the perfect thing, place or path to happiness, then to say simply that it does not matter if you get it or not.

One way around this trickiness is to keep a mantra in mind as you do this work that what you dream of, or perhaps, something even better is coming your way. Take time to meditate on what you want, then put yourself into the feeing place of something unknown but even better than you could possibly consider taking its place. It feels good, doesn't it?

Has this ever happened to you? Have you ever dreamed of achieving a thing only to have something better that you never could have imagined show up for you?

Sometimes the miracles of the Universe arrange *how* something will show up. Again, this is a reminder for you to loosen your grip on needing to know how things will manifest for you.

Your commitment to mastery of a lifestyle of success has the ability to yield tremendous results. Take ownership of the new you and then allow for something even better.

Chapter 17

Hear Yourself

If you hear a voice within you saying, you are not a painter, then by all means paint, and that voice will be silenced.

~Vincent Van Gogh - Prolific Painter, Expressive and Impulsive Emoter

One of the most crucial components to remember in all of the work that you are doing here, is that change happens on the inside. People who wait for the world around them to organize itself in a way that is pleasing to them are often disappointed, as success shines for them only occasionally and in a way that is truly outside of their control.

Let me ask you something. If you never reached the goals you set out for yourself but remained blissed out with happiness anyway, would that be okay with you? This, again, is part and parcel of letting go, but I am really asking you this so that you consider more deeply the fact that this journey toward greatness that you are on, is truly an inner game. You cannot expect the forces of other people and your environment to arrange themselves to create success for you. You can, however, expect change when you start from the inside.

Since this is an inner game, let us take a good, hard look at what goes on inside. That is, what plays in your head during the quiet moments?

Have you ever been driving or walking along, and in your head, you are replaying an argument? This time you are cleverer than before and you deliver all the witty comebacks and retorts that send your foe reeling. Or maybe you try out different phrases that would have stung deeper than what you actually said.

Perhaps it is an argument that is yet to come that has captured your attention. Maybe you are anticipating what will happen if you speak a certain way or bring a sticky point to someone who needs to be confronted.

Sometimes, people spend valuable time creating dialogue that is not even theirs - and never will be. But let's take a deep look at what this phenomenon really is and why it affects you so negatively.

First of all, if this is something that has not happened yet, or is something that has happened, but in a different way it is, by definition, *fiction.* Fiction pure and simple.

So, if you are going to use your creative forces for fiction, why on earth would you do it in a way that hurts you? I am sure that you are a very creative person. I think we all are in some way. If you are really *choosing* to deploy your creativity, please don't spend your energy creating negative scenarios in your head. It will only hurt you, even if you think that you are just preparing for what is to come.

Yes, it's true, creating negative fiction in your head does hurt you. Here are a few examples of the physical stress responses when you do this:

- increased heart rate
- muscle constriction and fatigue
- increased cortisol levels (stress hormone)
- decrease in ability to problem solve
- slower access to your executive brain
- lowered immune response

So, basically, fighting fiction in your head makes you dumb and weak.

Is this what you choose for yourself? You are not alone. We all do it in one form or another. In fact, during times of stress, some people actually become addicted to doing it, and will fall back on replaying negative scenarios over and over again.

This is only one type of self-talk that can get us into trouble. There are other versions of this disastrous scenario that look a little different, but affect you on the inside the same way. You need to ward yourself from these too.

The first of these is berating yourself after doing something wrong or silly. If, every time I make a mistake, I say to myself, "Merkel! You big idiot, what were you thinking?" After a time, my subconscious would hear those words said by my own mouth, heard in my own ears, and would start to believe the message, "I am an idiot."

Naturally, your brain will obey what it perceives is important. If you told it emphatically, over and over again that you were an idiot, or some rendition of stupidity, your brain would automatically compel you to behave in ways that would provide evidence to your brain that this is, indeed, true.

If you get nothing else out of this book, do this one thing for me- be kind to yourself. You need to be your own best friend and champion yourself to make any of this work. You need to love yourself always.

Your brain listens to your own voice above all others. Be careful how you use your voice, both out loud and in your own head, and if you are going to talk to yourself say things like:

"Hey Gorgeous!"

"Hi Handsome!"

"You're amazing at (fill in the blank)"

Or my personal favorite, "I'm a motherfucking rockstar"

Know what pumps you up and makes you feel good about yourself. Use that to replace some of the name-calling or shaming that might otherwise be going on in your head.

The second version similar to fighting in your head, is getting a bad case of the "*can't's*". It is a terrible illness that can stop even the heartiest among us in their tracks.

Saying, "I can't," either out loud or to yourself, provides clear and concise direction to your brain on exactly what you should continue to fail at.

For example, I used to believe that I was bad at parallel parking. I would routinely shy away from meeting friends downtown or at the very least, arrive a full half-hour early so that I could find a parking place that did not require me to parallel park. Because, you know, I told my brain that I couldn't do it.

One day, I realized that was a bunch of hooey. The only reason that I could not parallel park was that I had told myself a story about how hard it was and I refused even to practice. I decided I needed to change that. So, for a while, I allowed myself to be a learner. I allowed myself to giggle at mistakes I would make, and persevere through the learning process. I made myself find opportunities to work on it whenever I could. I began to insist that I meet friends and business associates downtown so that I could practice my new skill.

Do you know what happened? Duh! I became very proficient at parallel parking. These days it is second nature for me just as other areas of mastery are. The very first step in changing that about myself was to become aware of the story I was telling myself. With each retelling, my brain was embedding its instructions even deeper.

Do you have *can't's*? I am sure you do. We all have them and we all have the opportunity to begin telling ourselves we can. Write down in your journal, the places where the *can't's* slip in for you. See if there is a plan of action that you can deploy to overcome something that you previously thought you were bad at, or do not possess the necessary talent for.

If you do have to talk about it out loud with other people, try this technique on for size:

"I haven't yet learned how to parallel park, but I'm working on it."

Whatever you want to improve, people understand that you may be learning something new. In fact, you may even inspire someone else to take on one of their daunting tasks. What do you want to improve in your life and what kind of "I can" statements do you want to begin saying?

Chapter 18

What Would You Say?

My best friend is the one who brings out the best in me.

~Henry Ford – Tenacious Automobile Industrialist

The voices in our heads and the things we say to ourselves are not the only areas of discussion that we need to consider when we attempt a lifestyle of success mastery. The things we say in social groups, and anywhere someone else is listening is prime breeding ground for self-sabotage if we are not careful.

We have already talked about deflecting compliments. Remember how damaging it is to tell someone that the compliment they are giving you does not really belong to you? We forget how to receive goodness in our lives when we constantly and consistently push it away. There is a sister phenomenon that creeps into social settings that you need to be equally careful of.

Have you ever shown up to work, or any other social setting where people you know embark on their day and a familiar cultural drama of negativity unfolds? I call it trying to "Out-Crappy-Day" each other. It looks something like this:

Person 1: *"Oh my goodness, you won't believe the morning I just had. My alarm didn't go off and then, when I was rushing to get to work my heel broke and I spilled coffee down my shirt."*

Person 2: *"You think that's bad? This morning after realizing that I missed a deadline today, I left the house with just enough time to drop off my wife and the car wouldn't start."*

Person 3: *"Oh, that's nothing. Get this..."*

And they go on with a grisly tale that is the office equivalent of "hold my drink."

I know you know what I am talking about. Why do we do this? Every time I bring this up with people they always chuckle nervously because they know deep down that they have faithfully played out this script ever since they were young. We do it because we watched so many other people play it out before we were ever old enough to be included. I have even seen it done between strangers in lines at the grocery store.

Do you know some people who are "Out-Crappy-Day" champions? They thrive on winning every day. It is as if they stockpile their woes to tell the world what a crappy time they are having at life.

Seriously, have you ever stopped to wonder why we do this? It is for sympathy, surely, but when you really think about it, don't you wonder why we would participate in such a broadcasting of our incompetence?

What would happen if we did not participate? What would the dialogue look like if one of the participants in a group of complainers all of a sudden started talking about the things that they are grateful for or the blessings in their morning instead of the monsters out to get them?

It is likely that everyone would shame them in some underlying social way to indicate that they are not playing by the rules. But once you point out to the other participants in your game that your refusal to play by the rules is simply because you want to focus more on the positive, you will most likely find allies in this.

I truly believe that most of us do not really *want* to define our days through the lens of what is wrong with us. We simply lack the awareness of the impact our cultural interplay has on us. We have done it subconsciously for so long that we are participating habitually.

The next time this little tragedy plays out for you, with full expectations that you participate, feel free to interrupt the cycle by declaring your desire to frame your day differently. You do not need to put other people down for their participation because, well, that is not very positive now, is it? But it is okay to teach them an alternate way of participating in a cultural ritual.

Suggest that everyone show up with a check-in about what successes they had the previous day. Or, begin your time together with what you hope to achieve today. Either option is by far preferable than ritualizing negativity into your friendships.

Sometimes though, social talk can get in your way of success without other people even being present. Sadly, you can do this all on your own if you are not careful and paying attention to the words and phrases that you habitually say.

I once worked with a woman named Sarah who desperately wanted to thrive in her new business but things didn't seem to be working in her favor. In the process of going through the blueprint, and coaching her toward her lighthouse, I heard her say phrases that raised red flags. She would say things like:

"I don't need much money."

"I don't want to become too rich, because you know, rich people are bad."

"I bought myself a new car but I feel just awful about it."

"I certainly don't want to lose connection to people over money."

I learned a lot about her hidden beliefs through these phrases, and many more just like them. After probing further, I learned that in her family of origin she never had more than what she needed and sometimes barely that. Her father would justify their lack by saying things that vilified wealthy people. In her brain, there was a connection between doing evil things and being wealthy.

She also had a mistaken belief that people who had money were necessarily unhappy and disconnected. She was taught, from an early age, to distrust people with money and by extension, people who had nice things.

As a middle-aged woman with a family of her own, she was tired of just barely getting by and wanted to do nice things for her family. At the same time, she had a sound business plan to reach a higher level of wealth, but she could not seem to stop getting in her own way.

I asked her if she ever spoke these money-negative phrases to her friends and in social settings.

"All the time." She replied. "It's what we talk about, and I need to vent to my friends."

You see, it was her ongoing dialogue in social settings that solidified her limiting beliefs. Over and over again, her subconscious brain told her exactly why it would be a terrible thing if she were to begin making more than just enough money to get by. She was trapped by her own subconscious mind while she was trying desperately, on the conscious level, to change her circumstances through her business.

Sarah, like many of my clients, knows exactly what she needs to do to get out of the situation she is currently in. She has a good business brain and a plan for making it work. But for some reason, like many others in the same situation, she could not seem to get there on her own. It takes a lot for someone to admit that they may be holding themselves back, and even more for someone to actually *do* something about it. But if you can be brave enough to recognize that the way you talk about your plight in life may be the thing that is keeping you down, you can create a map towards change.

For Sarah, she needed examples and evidence for her brain to believe that people could be good *and* kind *and* wealthy at the same time. Her first obstacle was to overcome the idea that this was even possible. So, I had her start a collection.

I truly believe that if you want to find evidence of a new belief, no matter what that new belief is, you will find it. Evidence is everywhere.

I asked Sarah to find people in her life who were lovely *and* wealthy. Once she found one, she needed to hear all about their own money stories and then she needed to find another person. Then rinse and repeat until she had a nice collection of people who had positive wealth stories.

After a time, she had made some new, purposeful connections surrounding wealth and she had new ideas of her own of what her life could look like without sacrificing being a good person. Her business and life began to unfold in beautiful ways in the absence of sabotage. Her wealth blossomed and she enjoyed the luxury of things she really wanted. She also loved her new-found ability to give back. Sarah was finally in the position to become a philanthropist, a perk she loved and solidified her new beliefs that being wealthy could mean being a good human being.

For you, Dear Reader, I want you to hear yourself when you are chatting to your friends or colleagues. What phrases are your fallbacks? What do you say repeatedly? Do these words and phrases serve you or drag you under as you attempt to reach your lighthouse?

Take note of the things that come out of your mouth that are corroborated by others in your circle. Write them down in your journal and visit them from time to time for check-ups on their impact in your life. When you become aware of what you are doing, you can stop the negativity from coming to the surface by changing your story.

Chapter 19

Balanced Nutrition

Love can never have a negative effect, only a positive effect.

~Ziggy Marley – Reggae Artist and Fly Rasta

I bet you know the answer to my next question.

What happens to your body if you race around during the day with only time for a soda and a bag of chips to eat while driving to your next appointment?

It is conventional wisdom, after all. Nutrition is important, and we cannot neglect our bodies for very long before serious consequences befall our plans for success. Our poor attempts at "lunch" could be the very undoing of our afternoon as our bodies begin to crash and beg us for some proper fuel.

Sadly, while physical nutrition, or the kind we access through our mouths is very important, and is an integral part of any path toward success, it should not be done in the absence of mental nutrition.

I have often wondered why our culture readily accepts an understanding or even an admonishment of physical nutrition, to the point where it is actually taught in schools (thank goodness), but completely ignores the importance of knowing how to be mindful of what we allow access into our minds.

I would also like you to now take a rather complete inventory of what you let into your mind. And as you know by now, the state of your brain, and the level of thinking when you let information in, makes a huge difference in the results you experience.

This concept came into the forefront of my awareness many years ago, when my oldest son was in preschool and my youngest, an infant. I will admit to having limited patience of our Music Together CD's (don't know Music Together? Let this be a shameless plug for a great early childhood start to music!) and often reverted to my addiction to national news. This was all fine and dandy until the day that the small voice from a car seat in the back of my mini-van says, "Mommy, what does 'beheaded' mean?"

Well shit. What was I exposing my precious babies to? Why couldn't I be okay with another round of "Hello Everybody?" What were they picking up in their subconscious brains as I zoned out on my drive? What was I exposing my *own* subconscious mind to while I was zoned out? I felt horrible.

It was at that moment that I became painfully aware of what had access to my brain. Yes, I said that right, not what I had access to, but what had access to me. I suddenly saw it as an insidious worm that worked its way into my brain when I was not paying attention. I imagined the impact it had on me as well as my children.

The worst part of it was that while I was driving, a task I had moved from my conscious brain to my subconscious brain many years' prior, any information I put into my head had VIP access to being hard-wired to my belief systems. I was victim to the crap that I allowed in during the quiet times, and when I took the time to analyze exactly what that was, I was not at all happy about the content.

Think about the things that you see and hear at on a regular basis. Knowing what you do now about how your emotions create a one-way ticket to your subconscious brain, and also the ease of rewiring your brain while you are in the Alpha state, we can see that you may unwittingly be spending hours inputting negative beliefs into your brain without realizing it.

There are two exercises that I would like you to write down in your journal that will help you pay attention to your mental nutrition.

The first part of your next exercise is to create a list during the course of a week of every kind of information that you let into your brain. Next to each item you list, I want you to write the corresponding emotion that each entry evokes.

For instance, if you wake up in the morning and look at emails, I want you to write down the different themes that they represent. Then monitor the feelings inside you that each different theme begins to bring up in you.

You may have some emails that are sales solicitations. How do you really feel when you read them? Are you frustrated because you do not have money to buy new things? Are you happy about the thought of browsing through new shopping ideas? Do you feel overwhelmed by so many people trying to wrestle you out of your hard-earned cash?

Try to be as clear as possible about what comes up for you. You may even notice some statements that act as red-flags signifying potential areas of self-sabotage. Explore deeply and as thoroughly as you can even if it seems silly to be meditating on the feelings that an online retailer gives you. If it is something that you interact with every day, it could be adding to the deepening of a hidden belief that may be getting in your way of imprinting new and more powerful beliefs that lead to a higher level of success in your life.

Repeat this process for each segment of email you may receive: work, friends, professional development. Use this exercise as an excuse to clean the fluff out of your inbox that does not serve you.

Then move on to other areas of potentially unchecked media in your sphere. Do you use Facebook or any other type of social media? What kinds of stories or links show up in your feed? How do they make you feel? Here is a hint with this type of input: in particular, watch out for the feeling of indignation. It is one of the most insidious emotions out there, and it happens to be one of the more common feels you come across in social media land.

Have you ever seen the bumper sticker or slogan that reads, "if you're not outraged, you're not paying attention?" This makes me absolutely crazy (yes, I do see the irony here) that people are egging each other on to leave behind a feeling of centered peace in exchange for one that fosters blockages in every area of your life.

Let me be crystal clear here. There is nothing attractive, to the Universe or to other people, about someone who is outraged. This feeling is an absolute deal-breaker in the world of manifestation. Take everything I have said about thinking positively and vibrating on the frequency of what you want to heart, and put some faith into the process of positivity.

If you are actively trying to find new clients, or fix your relationship with your spouse, or lose 20 pounds, by fostering a new and improved level of understanding of possibility and opportunity, and at the same time you are spending time during your day working yourself into a lather about the current political situation or latest argument on media that you do not have anything to do with, you are driving with one foot on the gas and one on the brake at the same time.

This exercise is one of great importance when you are attempting to master the art of living a successful life. I am not saying that you cannot be an activist in any way and be successful at the same time. If activism in one area or another truly is your purpose, then go for it with gusto. Just remember to be *for* what you want instead of being against what you do not want. Many people make the ongoing mistake of putting all their attention on what they are fighting *against* instead of fighting for what they want to add into their lives. This is the same principle of focusing on your lack and getting more scarcity in your life versus focusing on what you are grateful for and then getting that and so much more, all while experiencing more happiness.

Looping back around to our exercise, continue on with every area of your life where information has access to your brain on a regular basis. Think about the people you surround yourself with, as we have discussed their impact on your growth and what you can do about it in chapter 11. Think also about the radio you listen to and the television you watch.

Think about your experiences on the internet and the news that you read.

Make sure everything within your control is doing something to *serve* your intentions rather than breaking down your potential of reaching them. You may realize that you have more control over your environment than you realize. All of a sudden you become a navigator with paddles in your boat instead of one without.

The second area of watching your mental nutrition involves what you let in when you are in an Alpha brain wave state. I mentioned above my experience of zoning out while listening to the radio, and this was very important to recognize as I was creating a fast channel into my subconscious as I did so. What areas of your life are you susceptible to rewiring your brain through the meditative process without your permission?

Do you come home after a long, exhausting day of work and turn on the boob-tube? Do you use television to "unwind" because it offers "mindless entertainment?"

I hear this one quite frequently and it worries me for the people who use this technique on a daily basis. Think about the brain wave that you are likely to be in as you relax deeply into your couch cushions, perhaps after a full meal, and shortly before you go to bed. What messages are you letting in during this time?

I should take this moment to discuss something that I find wildly prevalent in the tone of Western television, and that is the use of sarcasm.

While there are a few different forms of sarcasm, the most widely used is the one where people use thinly veiled insults with each other and call it funny. If someone's brain has high level access to snarkiness such as sarcastic television supplies, they become programmed for cynicism.

I have seen this happen over time with individuals who enter into phases of their lives where they let more "mind candy" television in, only to become more bitter and cynical in their day to day tasks. It is sad to watch, especially when it can be so easily avoided.

Do this same exercise in your journal about what kinds of shows you watch and monitor how they make you feel. Then, if you tend to watch movies or shows before you go to sleep add the category of what quality of sleep you had the night before. Rate your sleep in correlation to the content of what you watched and look for patterns that might suggest a programming shift.

What are your categories? Do you like zombie shows and murder mysteries? Or do you like romantic comedies and smart dialogue? Please know that I am not advocating for one genre over another. I simply care about what each does for you when you are vulnerable to self-sabotage because of it.

I, myself, am a huge fan of action and adventure films. Quite frankly, a good international espionage flick is my go-to genre when I have the choice. I also know that if I watch something like this right before I go to bed then I will struggle to sleep well all night long.

I have had clients do this exercise before who insist that their zombie-show habit does nothing to affect them adversely. Sadly, it is only because they have developed a new sense of what is normal that they do not recognize that anything might be amiss. It is only when they go without and chart the difference in quantifiable ways, such as how many times they woke up, or the quality of their sleep, that they recognize that their version of normal might not be very healthy.

Again, this is not me being anti-zombie. This is a friendly reminder, or a stern warning if you wish, that popular culture, while lots of fun, may not be doing you a service in the realm of living a successful life. Ultimately, you get to choose what you watch, but that is the whole point of this exercise. Choose wisely, and based on what you know about how your brain works and how you may be getting in your own way of success.

If you have a lighthouse to reach, by all means, clear the path before you if you can. Recognize where you may be laying your own obstacles before you and wean yourself from the habits of inhibiting or slowing your own success.

When you master your level of thinking, you can let the good stuff in, keep the crap at bay, and own the success you bring into your life.

~

My deepest hope for you is that armed with enhanced confidence and the tools to invite lasting success into your life, you embark on a journey of change that brings you everlasting joy and abundance. Once you use the techniques from this book to grow your results in one area of your life, hit repeat and do it again. There are no limits to what this work can do for you, so I want you to try your boundaries. See what's possible for you today. Then, when you prove to yourself that positive change is available to you, do it again.

I love to hear about my readers' successes. If you will, please take the time to reach out to me to share all about your *"You're not going to believe what happened..."* moments. I will believe it and I'll share in your celebration.

Afterword

I'm a Success Coach. It's what I do.

I would not be living my own truth if I did not add a plug in here for you to get your own coach.

Yes, you have valuable tools here at your fingertips that you can implement today to experience change in your life. Also, I want you to know how rich the experience can be when you work with someone who can see your life from the etic view, or the outsider's perspective.

I find it interesting that people who want to excel in their lives in sport think nothing of hiring a coach. It is a cultural norm, and in fact, society would question your commitment to your craft if you tried to be serious in sport without one. We have never heard of an Olympian, a World Champion, or even a state level competitor without a coach. In fact, coaches are so valuable in guiding someone through the struggles of learning sport that we hire them for our children, thus enculturating them with the importance of coaching in all of sports' endeavors.

Why is it then, generally speaking, that coaching has been left only to CEO's of Fortune 500 companies in the success realm?

Luckily, we are starting to experience a shift in this mistaken way of thinking. Some companies are now prioritizing coaching for their upper level management to better their outcomes.

But for someone unattached to a forward-thinking organization such as this, it is up to them to recognize the importance of receiving guidance and support as they attempt to break barriers and reach new shores with new lighthouses.

I recommend it highly to anyone who is serious about change in their lives. With coaching comes accountability. Through the use of pattern recognition, a coach can see and understand what appears too normal for you to see. They can help unravel mysteries that may have plagued you for years.

Yes, continue to read books such as this, and attend workshops if you can. Please know that there is nothing quite as powerful as getting a trained set of eyes on your own unique opportunities. Through coaching you have the chance of experiencing true, quantum leaps in your projects, your goals, and in reaching any lighthouse you wish.

For more information about working with me or one of my Licensed Internal Alchemie Coaches, please visit alchemieacademy.com or email us at info@alchemieacademy.com

To Your Abundance,
Jenean

Acknowledgements

This book, or the concepts from it, wouldn't exist without my boys: Scott, Ethan and Finn. I couldn't ask for a more supportive and smartly-witted family. I love you boys with all my heart and am filled with joy and gratitude for you every day.

Thank you to my wonderful Lab-Mates who aid me by providing an air of creativity on a daily basis. Julie Sullivan and Lara Gamora from Shine Creative Industries, and Mary Ross from Mary Ross Design. I am blessed to have them as my everyday partners in work and play.

Thank you to my dear Holes, who encouraged me along every step of the way during my book-writing shenanigans: My derby wifey, Goldie Gloxxx; plus, Mo U. Down; Skary B. Cheezus; Sinister SnOman; Taco Bruiseday; and Twilight Chaos. Your friendship, advice and ability to go day-drinking on a Tuesday during this growth process was exactly what I needed.

Thank you also to Laura Kelly and Inda Eaton. Even though you ladies are far away, your enduring friendship and sparkle inspires me to raise the expectations I have of myself. Thank you.

ABOUT THE AUTHOR

Jenean Merkel Perelstein lives in Flagstaff, Arizona with her husband, Scott, her two sons, and her Labrador, Buzi. She is happiest when she is helping people get out of their own way and stand in their strength.